Better Homes and Gardens.

IDEAS & HOW-TO

Storage & Organizing

John Wiley & Sons, Inc.

IDEAS & HOW-TO

Storage & Organizing

For general information about our other products and services, please contact our Customer Care Department within the United States at (800) 762-2974, outside the United States at (317) 572-3993 or fax (317) 572-4002.

Wiley also publishes its books in a variety of electronic formats. Some content that appears in print may not be available in electronic books. For more information about Wiley products, visit our web site at www.wiley.com.

ISBN 978-0-470-48804-1

Printed in the United States of America

10 9 8 7 6 5 4

Contents

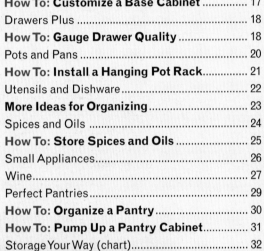

 # Welcome

If you open a closet that bursts with clothes, can never find the right spice for your favorite recipe, and spend more time clearing the kitchen table than eating on it, *Ideas & How-To: Storage & Organizing* is the path to your success. This book provides practical solutions to common organizational problems, addressing everything from organizing closets and entryways to finding space for hobby supplies. The concept is simple: Commit to cleaning one small space at a time—a drawer, an armoire, a closet. In a few months all your organizational woes will be behind you and friends will envy your storage savvy. Sound appealing? Turn the page and get organized!

Open storage rises to "enlightened" heights. Doors with glass inserts adorn the fronts and backs of the cabinets installed above the peninsula and over the kitchen windows, mingling a beautiful backyard view with the sparkle of glassware.

Crown molding that tops two ready-made bookshelves draws the picture of a built-to-fit corner. The cabinets provide storage for books and hobby supplies (hidden inside lidded baskets) and show off a collection of birdhouses.

1 Kitchens and

Efficient storage, suited to your needs, is essential in the kitchen. Busy cooks want pots, tools, and spices within reach. Busy individuals want well-organized pantries. And dishware for everyone should be as easy to put away as it is to retrieve.

Pantries

Open and Closed Storage

If you feel strongly about light and like to see your dishes at a glance, your choice is either open shelves or cabinets with glass doors. Open shelves and clear glass doors allow you to quickly find what you're looking for while revealing the colors and shapes of your belongings.

One caveat: Open storage demands that you keep items within the cabinets or on the shelves in an orderly manner, since they are always in view. If you like the idea of a certain amount of color and shape remaining visible but don't want to worry about keeping cabinet interiors tidy, consider doors with translucent or decorative glass panels that partially obscure what's inside. Try panels with seeded glass or rice paper laminated between glass panes.

For those who prefer clean countertops and minimal accessories on view, closed cabinet storage is for you. To prevent overwhelming the kitchen with cabinetry, install upper cabinets at varying heights and pull a few lower cabinets forward (or select some that are deeper than others) for visual variety. You may also want to include one or two cabinets with glass doors and lighted interiors to offer a resting place for the eyes as well as display space for a few treasures.

No need for lighted cabinetry in this kitchen. Glass-front, see-through units mounted in front of windows create a sun-from-behind design while spotlighting the beauty of glassware on display.

Cabinetry that resembles a breakfront, hutch, or armoire is the ultimate in stylish storage. White dishes, which are clearly visible through windowpane glass doors (and artfully displayed against beaded board), are easily unloaded onto the nearby island. Feel free to mix antiques with custom-built cabinets.

Three tiers of white beaded-board door cabinets encase this butler's pantry in beautiful storage space. Upper cabinets with glass door panels display seldom-used tureens that provide visual variety. Open shelves on the left keep cookbooks at hand.

HOW TO ARRANGE VISIBLE STORAGE

Glass-door cabinets and open shelves provide a full and easy view of kitchen dishware, dry goods, and other essentials. Observe these tips for a tidy, attractive look:

- **Consider height.** Store taller items at the back of the shelf or cabinet with smaller things at the front.
- **Sort by color.** For decorative impact consider grouping dishware (and even dry goods) in collections with similar color or colors that complement one another.
- **Watch the labels.** Keep labels turned outward and keep boxes and cans lined up—especially on open shelves.
- **Include baskets.** Use wire, woven, or plastic baskets to store smaller and/or less attractive items.

Narrow shelves, when placed near a cooktop, are handy for holding herbs, oils, and spices. They are easy to see and reach during food preparation.

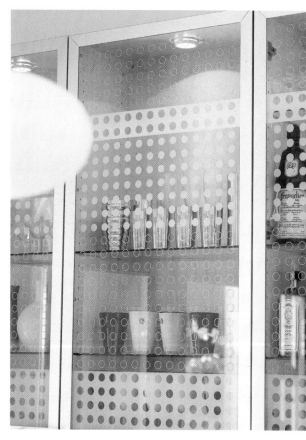

Decorative frosted glass on cabinet doors allows for see-through storage of dishes, glassware, or food items. Colors and shapes remain visible but the contents don't have to remain as tidy as things stored inside a cabinet with a clear-glass door.

Besides their fashionable presentation, cube-style open shelves ensure logical organization for often-used items. Attractive baskets hold linens and smaller items for a clutter-free appearance.

 # Island Ways

A center island is probably the most-requested storage feature in a kitchen. It's little wonder, with the abundance of storage, seating, and work surface a single island can offer. Make the best use of counterspace by including a sink or cooktop. Below the countertop consider a combination of cabinets, drawers, and open shelves. Be careful to size your island so there is plenty of walkway space between it and perimeter cabinets. Most rules of thumb suggest at least 42 inches—48 inches is even better, especially when more than one cook shares the work core.

A useful island base includes a variety of storage options. This one has it all, including room for a large collection of cookbooks. The long shelf below the countertop is perfect for storing two oversize bowls.

HOW TO CUSTOMIZE A DRESSER

If you're shopping for an island, you might find what you need at a flea market or a garage sale. Sturdy old dressers can have both personality and potential.

1. Sand, prime, and paint. Remove drawers and hardware. Then sand all the surfaces and wipe away sanding residue with a tack cloth. Apply a coat of primer; let dry. Brush or roll one or two coats of color.

2. Replace knobs. Select and install new knobs or drawer pulls to complement the rest of your kitchen.

3. Top it off. This bureau already featured a marble top, but you could add a countertop made of solid surfacing, laminate, tile, stainless steel, butcher block, or another material that you prefer.

4. Accessorize. The sides of this island become storage workhorses with the addition of large hooks for utensils and a holder for paper towels.

The knobs above appear to open three cabinet doors. Actually the drawer is a single pullout with three bins for recyclables and dog food.

1

2

3

4

Someone else's trash could become your island treasure. Scour flea markets and garage sales to find old treasures or farm tables that you can retrofit as an island. If the one you find doesn't have wheels, add casters to make it mobile.

Making the Most of an Island

Make your kitchen island convenient and practical.

- If a cooktop is part of the plan, a downdraft vent or a hood suspended from the ceiling is a necessity. You may want your island to feature a sink and/or food prep space instead. If the sink is the only one in your kitchen, it must be deep enough (and the faucet high enough) to wash large pots. Also consider equipping it with a garbage disposer.
- Each end of the cooktop should be bordered with at least 12-inch-wide runs of countertop.
- Electrical outlets located on the side of the island—instead of on top—help prevent electrical shock.
- Shelf space for cookbooks and collectibles dresses up otherwise bare sides. A built-in TV works here too, especially if it faces the family room. Even a microwave, installed at an ideal height for the kids, is convenient for heating up after-school snacks.
- Extend the countertop or recess cabinets to allow for leg space.
- Seating across from the cooktop is great for a quick meal; make sure the countertop area between the chairs and cooktop measures at least 12 inches.
- Rounded corners help protect children from injury.
- Countertop material can vary from the rest of your kitchen's counters as long as it's harmonious with the room's overall design. You may want to splurge on solid

This center island began as a stock base cabinet and is customized with add-on shelves and beaded board. Bins tuck into shelves on this end to store potatoes, onions, and squash. A shelf on the opposite end of the island holds the microwave oven.

HOW TO CUSTOMIZE A BASE CABINET

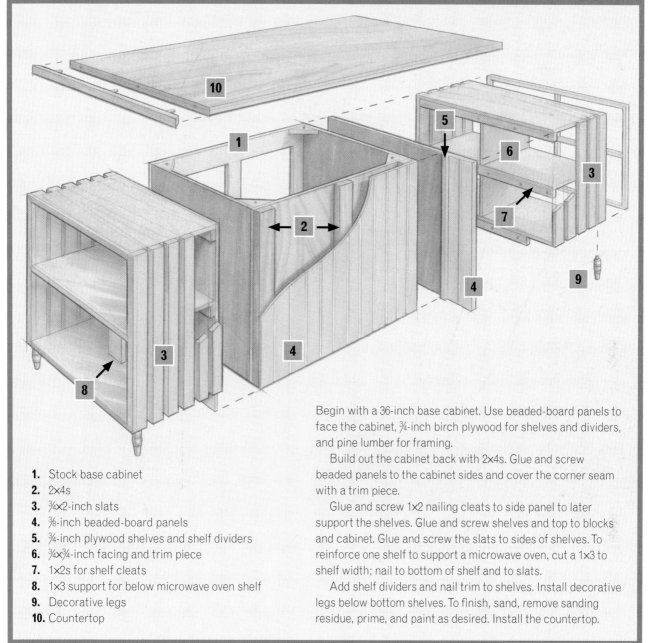

1. Stock base cabinet
2. 2×4s
3. ¾×2-inch slats
4. ⅜-inch beaded-board panels
5. ¾-inch plywood shelves and shelf dividers
6. ¾×¾-inch facing and trim piece
7. 1×2s for shelf cleats
8. 1×3 support for below microwave oven shelf
9. Decorative legs
10. Countertop

Begin with a 36-inch base cabinet. Use beaded-board panels to face the cabinet, ¾-inch birch plywood for shelves and dividers, and pine lumber for framing.

Build out the cabinet back with 2×4s. Glue and screw beaded panels to the cabinet sides and cover the corner seam with a trim piece.

Glue and screw 1×2 nailing cleats to side panel to later support the shelves. Glue and screw shelves and top to blocks and cabinet. Glue and screw the slats to sides of shelves. To reinforce one shelf to support a microwave oven, cut a 1×3 to shelf width; nail to bottom of shelf and to slats.

Add shelf dividers and nail trim to shelves. Install decorative legs below bottom shelves. To finish, sand, remove sanding residue, prime, and paint as desired. Install the countertop.

surfacing material, for instance, and use laminate on other countertops. A butcher-block countertop is ideal for food preparation; granite works well for baking tasks.

- Pendant or recessed fixtures installed above the island direct adequate light onto work surfaces.
- Your island cooktop or sink can be part of your work triangle, but be sure it's at least 42 inches from any adjacent cabinets, tables, or appliances. Expand that width to a roomier 48 to 64 inches if two or more will work simultaneously.
- For general food preparation, set the countertop 36 inches high, the same as most other kitchen countertops.

If you'll use your island for baking—rolling out dough and hand mixing, for instance—drop it to 32 or 33 inches and you'll find the handwork less fatiguing. For snack bar purposes, the standard 36-inch height accommodates most kitchen stools. If you prefer bar-height seating, set the counter at 42 to 45 inches; for table height, lower it to 28 to 32 inches. Or combine a couple of countertop heights for a multipurpose island.

- If you choose an enclosed cabinet base, the standard drawer and cupboard storage options apply. For an open design, large shelves are ideal for holding pots, pans, and large bowls.

Drawers Plus

Designers love to infuse the kitchen with lots of drawers for a reason: You can open them in one smooth motion and see all the contents from front to back. Drawers and pullouts can be used liberally throughout your kitchen; the secret is to size them for what you want to store—deep drawers for bulky items, such as pots and pans, and shallow depths for silverware and knives, for example. Specialty dividers help organize lids, trays, and the ubiquitous "junk drawer." The first step is to consider all the things you want to store in the kitchen and plan drawer and pullout storage accordingly.

HOW TO GAUGE DRAWER QUALITY

Can your cabinet drawers and pullouts take what you dish out? Few components take a harsher beating. If you're buying new cabinets, check the warranty. Insist on high-quality metal glides with nylon rollers or ball bearings, and a 75-pound load rating or better. Open a drawer an inch; it should close on its own. Open it again, this time to the stops. The drawer should open smoothly without excessive side play, then stop before it exits the cabinet so it can't accidentally spill its contents. Other signs of quality drawer construction include a solid-wood face, ⅝ inch or thicker sides, a plywood bottom panel, and strong corner joints that are either doweled or dovetailed. Avoid sides that are simply stapled and glued together.

Unwieldy serving platters are easier to handle when stored in a tall, narrow pullout in this peninsula. The dishwasher in close proximity is an efficiency bonus.

This pullout offers an old-fashioned solution for storing bread—the drawer box features a pierced metal lid that allows ventilation. The lid slides back to access the contents of the drawer.

Compartmentalized drawers keep items separated. These stainless-steel dividers ease sorting of flatware and utensils and can be quickly wiped off or safely cleaned in the dishwasher.

Even a sliver of undercabinet space can be put to work from front to back with a multilevel pullout. This two-tier unit frees up counterspace by stowing idle appliances and other small cooking gadgets.

Toe-kicks are notoriously wasted spaces but not in this kitchen. Located in the island toe-kick, this kitty drawer pulls out at feeding time to expose pet food and water dishes.

Pots and Pans

In most kitchens pots and pans are used daily. Their bulky construction means they take up more space than most items, so they can be a challenge to store. Some cooks love to see every pot and pan they own and want to be able to reach and grab at a moment's notice. Pot racks meet these desires with style, proudly displaying a cook's collection. Ceiling-mount racks protect cookware from getting banged and scratched against each other. They also let chefs grab what they need in a motion that's easy on the back.

Some cooks, on the other hand, prefer to have their pots and pans tucked away in neat stacks with lids nearby.

Pullouts, drawers, and pullout shelves, which show everything from front to back, are the solution. In order to safely load concealed storage with heavy pots and pans, choose units that are well constructed from solid wood and feature fine-quality glides.

Whichever storage strategy you prefer—out of sight or in full view—there's an efficient and attractive means for meeting your needs.

A bar-style rack mounted on the backsplash behind the range puts four or five favorite pans on display. This type of storage eliminates the need to reach up or to bend down to retrieve pots and pans. For best visual effect, keep the pans polished.

If you prefer to see your pots and pans but don't want them in full view, store them on an open shelf. A shelf under this table-style island steers clutter out of sight lines.

Extra deep and wide units reveal a double layer of storage. The deeper bottom half is ideal for bulky pots and pans while the shallower upper pullout keeps lids tidy.

HOW TO INSTALL A HANGING POT RACK

Decorative pot racks are a great way to use the empty space over an island or stove.

You'll find many styles available online and in kitchen-supply stores. Hanging a rack will take only a couple of hours at the most.

1. Locate the joists in the ceiling using a stud finder.
2. As much as possible, match the locations of the ceiling hooks with the dimensions of the pot rack so that the chains will hang straight down.
3. For each ceiling hook drill a pilot hole. Screw the ceiling hook into the joist by inserting a screwdriver into it sideways and turning until the flange of the hook touches the ceiling.
4. Cut two to four sections of chain (depending on the style of the rack) so that each length has the same number of links. Attach the chain to the pot rack. With a helper lift the rack and hang the chains on the ceiling hooks.

If you love to collect cookware and can't bear to tuck it away, use a ceiling-mounted pot rack. Some units include lighting for a double-duty benefit.

# Utensils and Dishware

Utensils and dishware introduce armloads of items that beg for an orderly existence. For easy retrieval group flatware and cooking utensils together by type and locate them close to where they're needed—where you dine and near the stove or food preparation stations. While flatware is often stowed in a drawer, you must decide whether to keep cooking utensils in view or in closed storage. Similarly dishes may be too pretty to store behind closed doors. If so consider open racks or shelves behind glass doors. Regardless of the type of storage you decide upon for utensils and dishware, it's a good idea to locate both within a few steps of the dishwasher so pieces can be quickly unloaded and put away.

Wooden dividers keep a large quantity of flatware in order inside this deep drawer. The pieces are stored with handles pointing up for safe and easy retrieval.

A plate rack mounted in front of a window does little to obstruct a kitchen with a view. Sunlight filters through the storage piece and highlights the colorful dishware.

Wooden pegs placed strategically in a deep drawer keep dishes organized. Arrange the pegs to custom-fit your dishware.

MORE IDEAS FOR ORGANIZING

- Place dishware in cabinets or racks close to where you dine and near the dishwasher. Store infrequently used items, such as gravy boats and cake stands, elsewhere or up high, keeping valuable, easy-to-reach kitchen space for everyday needs.
- Store plasticware for kids in reachable lower cabinets with pullout shelving. That way your kids can learn to help set the table and put away clean dishes from the dishwasher.
- For extra storage consider space-saving furnishings such as banquettes with hinged tops. Such space works well for platters, trays, chafing dishes, extra pitchers, and tiered serving pieces you use only for special gatherings.

Knives in slots at the back of the cutting board are protected, keep fingers safe, and are easy to reach during food preparation. Slots in various widths cover a variety of knife sizes and styles.

Spices and Oils

Heat, light, and moisture are the enemies of dried spices. Heat causes flavor loss, light fades colors, and moisture causes ground spices to cake. When evaluating your spice collection, put your senses to work. Use sight to assess the vibrancy of spices and herbs; when the color fades, usually the flavor does too. Smell crushed spices or herbs in your hand; if the aroma is weak, replace them. Taste them too; if the flavor is weak, replace.

- Keep spices away from heat, moisture, and sunlight. Don't store spices and herbs over the stove, dishwasher, or sink, or near a window. Store in tightly closed containers.
- Use a dry measuring spoon in containers; moisture will cause deterioration.
- Store red peppers—paprika, chili powder, red pepper—in the refrigerator to retain color and freshness.

- Monitor the age of spices and herbs by putting the date they're first opened on the container with a felt-tip pen.
- Look for a series of black numbers and letters on the bottom or side of the spice container (on dry-seasoning packet mixes, the numbers and letters are pressed into the edge of the packaging). The first number indicates the year. If the number is 7, the product was packaged in 2007. The second character identifies the month alphabetically, as in "A" for January or "F" for June. Some packaging indicates a "best if used by" date.
- Instead of sprinkling spices directly from the bottle over a steaming pot, measure spices into another container then add them to the pot. Steam that gets into the spice container hastens flavor loss.

Designate a drawer near the cooktop for storing spices. Add a special insert that keeps jars tilted so the labels are easy to read. When you cook, slip the drawer out of the glides and set it on the countertop, then return the drawer when you're done.

HOW TO STORE SPICES

Here are some guidelines for the shelf life of spices that are properly handled.

Spices
    Ground—two to three years
    Whole—three to four years
    Herbs—one to three years
    Seeds—three to four years
Seasoning blends—one to two years
Extracts—four years

It's OK to think small when it comes to spices. Claim even the thinnest of spaces, such as the end of an island or the back of the counter, and you'll better see what's on hand.

HOW TO STORE OILS

Cooking oils can become rancid when exposed to heat, light, and oxygen. Since heat in a kitchen tends to rise, the bottom drawers offer cooler storage. One tip: Bottles are heavy; be sure to select high-quality heavy-duty glides so the drawers are easy to open and close.

Two shallow niches below an island countertop—one with a door and the other open—are just right for one-jar-deep spice storage. Oils are stowed on the bottom shelf where heat is less likely to damage the contents.

Small Appliances

Store small appliances according to how you use them. If you use the appliance daily and have sufficient space, keep it on the counter. For infrequently used appliances, a space outside the main work core, such as on a kitchen cart or behind closed pantry doors, will keep them hidden but accessible. Standard cabinet sizes can handle most small appliances, and accessories such as roll-out shelves and raised platforms can aid in lifting those that are heavy. An outlet inside an appliance garage puts power where you need it. Another tip is to create convenient stations for appliances that are used at the same time, such as a beverage station with a coffeemaker, a coffee grinder, and an espresso machine.

An "appliance garage" makes good use of the space between upper and lower cabinets. A tambour door doesn't swing out and therefore doesn't interfere with items on the counter. An electrical outlet allows appliances to be easily plugged in and ready for use.

Bulky, seldom-used appliances, such as this bread maker, store out of the way on the bottom rack of a rolling cart. The cart rolls into an undercounter alcove when not in use.

Special hardware makes it possible to store a heavy-duty mixer on a cabinet shelf. Open the cabinet doors and pull the shelf up and out to bring the mixer to user-friendly height. Include an outlet at the back of the cabinet so the mixer is ready to use.

 # Wine

Temperature changes, light, insufficient humidity, and excess movement are all enemies of good wine. Avoid these conditions to preserve and store your wine. Your kitchen—the most common place for drinking and storing—is fine for short-term storage of inexpensive wines. Just keep the wine out of areas that undergo drastic temperature fluctuations, such as the top of the refrigerator or near the stove. Built-in wine racks under counters and/or islands or between studs work best when space is tight. They also keep wine tilted, so the cork remains moist and air won't seep in and ruin the flavor. Bottles can be stored upright but only for short periods of time. Store wines by category (reds, whites, dessert wines) so you can quickly find the perfect vintage. Then organize them by maturation date so you'll be able to drink the wine at its peak of flavor.

Wine enthusiasts may want to invest in a refrigerated wine cabinet. (The best temperature for storing wine is between 50°F and 60°F with 60 to 70 percent humidity.) Most refrigerated cabinets come in freestanding or undercounter models and hold a minimum of 24 bottles.

Refrigerated coolers are specially designed for keeping wine at the right temperature and humidity. Store wine bottles on their sides so their corks stay moist.

This well-planned pantry handles a lot more than food. Drawers, shelves, and even the door house dining essentials, while the countertop stores oft-used small appliances. Electrical outlets inside the pantry allow cooks to use the appliances where they rest. Drawers offer easy access and keep items from being lost or forgotten in the back of a pantry shelf.

Perfect Pantries

According to a survey by the National Association of Home Builders, 85 percent of respondents included a walk-in pantry on their kitchen wish list. Fortunately this much-sought-after storage space is no longer considered a high-end amenity. And you don't need a huge kitchen to incorporate a pantry (walk-in or otherwise). Specialty pantry cabinets that store an abundance of goods are available. Creative design can transform small recesses, unused corners, broom closets, and otherwise wasted space into a walk-in style pantry.

To get the most out of your pantry, opt for adjustable shelving so you can adapt the space to changing storage needs. The shelves should stand no higher than 7 feet off the floor—the height most people can safely reach from a step stool. If the shelves are extra deep (more than 12 inches), consider a roll-out unit for easier access to items stored toward the back.

Remember there's no law that says pantries are only for storing food. Feel free to keep linens handy by draping them over mounted dowel rods in a cabinet or hanging them from pants hangers on a standard closet rod. Use vertical dividers to store bulky platters and cookie sheets.

You might be surprised where you can fit a pantry. Once a doorway into a bathroom, this shallow pantry was constructed to fill the opening. A screen door lends a playful touch and keeps the contents on view.

Use shelves for storing sets of china and plastic drawer dividers for holding flatware.

A pantry can be a working space as well. Free counterspace by installing electrical outlets in the pantry for using countertop appliances such as coffeepots, stand mixers, and food processors. If you have the space, consider creating a special work zone, such as a baking center with a pullout mixer stand or a beverage center with open wine storage and handy pullout shelving. With the addition of a sink and countertop, you can enjoy an old-fashioned butler's pantry, an annex that eases preparation, serving, and cleanup chores.

However simple or elaborate the design, good organization is the key to an efficient pantry. If there's no method to your storage madness, the pantry can easily turn from efficient annex to cluttered catchall.

Reminiscent of an old general store, glass jars and harvest bushels keep this pantry well organized. Clear or open containers make it easy to inventory your supplies and know when you're running out of a specific food or drink.

HOW TO ORGANIZE A PANTRY

Follow this strategy to conquer clutter in a food pantry cabinet or walk-in:

- **Empty the pantry.** Check labels to see if any food is past its expiration date. Also throw away items that no one likes or that are unlikely to be eaten.
- **Sort the items.** Separate food items into categories, such as vegetables, pastas, soups, and oils. Turn items so labels face outward and position on shelves with the tallest items at the back.
- **Reduce the clutter.** Snack bags and small packages, such as instant spice mixes, look messy and their labels are difficult to read. Instead store these items in clear plastic containers that stack. Flip-top lids work particularly well.

Coordinated baskets organize staples and produce in this tidy walk-in pantry. Most basket ends have hand grips for easy transport to the counter or table. Open shelves make selecting ceramics and dinnerware a breeze. Plastic bins and containers are storage-friendly pantry alternatives.

HOW TO PUMP UP A PANTRY CABINET

Deck out the interior of a wooden four-door pantry cabinet so it serves multiple functions.

1. Add a pegboard. Cut a piece of pegboard to fit the recessed portion of the door interior. Attach the pegboard to a lath frame with glue and staples. Then secure the pegboard to the door with wood glue. Clamp until dry.

2. Roll on a chalkboard. Use a foam roller to apply latex primer to the recessed portion of the pantry cabinet door interior; let dry. Use a clean foam roller to apply one or more coats of chalkboard paint. Allow the chalkboard to dry before use as recommended by the paint manufacturer.

3. Produce a place for pinups. Using a straightedge and a utility knife, trim a sheet of adhesive-back cork to fit the recessed portion of the door interior. Peel off the backing and adhere the cork to the door. Use pushpins to hold tickets, paint chips, lists, and other items in place until you need them.

4. Bring order with containers. Purchase plastic and glass containers for easy-to-see, tidy storage of pastas, cereal, sugar, flour, and other staples.

5. Create magnetic display space. Purchase a galvanized sheet-metal panel from a home center. Have the center cut the piece to size. You may also want to bend the sharp edges under. Secure the metal to the door using an adhesive formulated for wood and metal. Clamp until dry.

STORAGE YOUR WAY

As you design your kitchen storage and life changes, convenience is key. Here's a guide to storage through the stages of life.

	CABINETS	ACCESSORIES
Solo Act You often cook for one but still believe your kitchen should be efficient and well-equipped for get-togethers.	Reduced-depth cabinets allow units to stack without reducing counter work area. Roll-out trays make contents in base cabinets more accessible. Top-hinged wall cabinets occupy less aisle space than those with side-hinged doors. A base cabinet on casters can double as a mobile island or a handy serving cart. Doorless cabinets display small collections.	Wall-mount grids, pegboard, and rail systems keep frequently used ingredients and utensils handy. Adjustable dividers make the most of limited drawer space. Tiered stands maximize cabinet interiors' storage of canned goods. Instead of a hanging rack, consider a pot rail mounted to the wall or an end cabinet.
Couple/No Kids Maintain comfort in your shared space by planning smart, flexible storage that simplifies tandem meal preparation and party prep.	An angled drawer insert, a door-mount rack, or undercabinet shelves organize spices. Tambour-door cabinets hide blenders, coffee grinders, and other small appliances and keep countertops clear. An island with a sink or cooktop creates a second workstation; buy duplicate food-prep basics and provide a backup wastebasket.	Convert an armoire to a bar cabinet by mounting a wine rack inside. Or hang a wine rack on a wall or stand it on the countertop. Freestanding wire shelves showcase colorful canisters, dinnerware, serving pieces, and table linens. Baskets and oversize wood bowls corral fresh fruits and vegetables.
Family Affair Ensure a tidy and safe culinary hub with a design that keeps items handy and helps young ones pitch in.	A full-height pantry stocks staples and paper goods. A below-counter niche for the microwave oven allows kids to heat snacks without climbing or reaching. Countertop heights of 32 or 28 inches suit shorter helpers; a slide-out platform in the toe-kick gives them a boost. Tray dividers and bulk-ingredient drawers cater to bakers. Choose kid-friendly finishes that clean easily.	If desk space is nonexistent, install a pull-down message center near the phone. A pull-down knife rack keeps cutlery out of toddlers' reach. Turntables minimize disarray inside cabinets. Coated-wire carts are light enough for kids to maneuver. Baskets, bins, and jars store after-school snacks and homework and crafts project needs.
Empty Nesters Your dream kitchen is the one you can use for years to come. Blend accessibility, personality, and hospitality.	An island and barstools just outside the work core create a gathering spot for dinner guests. Roll-out drawers and trays and pop-up mixer stands reduce bending and lifting. Open shelves display cookbook spines like artwork. A cutting board or slide-out table adds a sit-down work surface. Drawers on base cabinets are more efficient and accessible than doors—especially from a wheelchair.	It's a return to the basics—but not to a budget—with accessories that are scaled down for a party of two. Pick top-of-the-line units that easily store and are dishwasher-safe. Consider weeding out the clutter of little-used items, moving them to a separate storage unit in the basement or garage.

FOOD

Cooking for one serves up its own challenges but that shouldn't stop you from exploring your taste bud temptations. Learn basic food-organizing principles (group by type in stackable sealed containers) that set you off on a surefire path to a well-honed pantry. If a night of cooking leaves you with leftovers, freeze them or store up to three days in the refrigerator.

Dinner parties are a regular occurrence in many couples' social lives, so you'll want plenty of pantry space to accommodate specialized ingredients. Continue to include easy-to-make meals and convenience food on your shopping lists for those long workdays.

Use clear plastic containers to organize food, allowing family members to easily see what's available. Create a kid-happy food zone: Stash healthy items in snack-size containers within easy reach, allowing kids to help themselves to both room-temperature and chilled items. If children are old enough and space allows, a lower-height microwave oven allows them to heat food on their own.

Nurture your food favorites but don't limit your palate. Keep the pantry stocked with plenty of easy-to-reach items in clear containers. Food needs will probably begin to decrease as kids leave the house, so don't overbuy and keep your shelves streamlined and clutter-free.

BAKING/COOKING

Review your pots and pans: Include large and small saute pans and large and small cooking pots with lids as starter cooking sets. Stash cookie sheets and lids with upright dividers to max out minimal cabinet space. Avoid buying supplies for cookie baking in bulk; the space sacrifice isn't worth the extra 5 pounds of flour.

Take time to stock a wide range of baking and cooking items. Round out your cake pans with both 8- and 9-inch versions, and add another midsize saute pan to your collection. Test out beyond-the-basic appliances, such as a juicer, blender, or top-notch food processor.

If a cooktop on an island is part of your kitchen design, include a raised backsplash, or ledge, at the back to protect anyone at the snack bar side from hot splatters. Folding step stools bring kids up to helping height but stash easily in a pantry closet. Remember to go vertical: Organize cookie sheets, cutting boards, and baking pans upright to max out space.

If pots and pans have begun to show wear and tear, consider replacing them with a few high-quality items that accommodate cooking and baking for two. Eliminate little-used large-scale appliances such as roasters and chafing dishes or move them to a storage spot outside the daily-use kitchen cabinets.

DISHES

Time to toss the paper plate bonanza that got you through your college years. Build your collection by starting with basics: eight large and small plates, bowls, and coffee cups in a plain color and pattern. Include a simple silverware set for eight, too, as well as basic serving bowls, platters, and utensils in any must-have list. Check for dishwasher- and microwave-safe ratings.

Expand your dishware repertoire past boring white with a collection of special-occasion items—great wineglasses, serving platters, even a set of china. Group similar collections for visual and physical accessibility, allowing you to see what you have and use what you see.

Stash rarely used items at head height or above and keep often-used dishes right around waist level. Devote one cabinet to plastic dishes, glasses, and utensils so kids can help themselves. You'll likely have more than one set of dishes, so consider a stand-alone unit in the kitchen or dining room to stash special-occasion items.

Transport once-a-year china or fine items to a spot in a dining room armoire. Better yet place your favorite fine china in a handy spot and use it often. If you're downsizing and moving, consider donating mismatched serving pieces to charity.

2 Entries, Mudrooms

Boots, shoes, jackets, backpacks, sporting equipment, and laundry are just a few of the items that clutter hardworking utility areas on a daily basis. Bring these catchall rooms back into order with a few fail-safe strategies and you'll spend less time picking up and more time doing what you love.

& Laundries

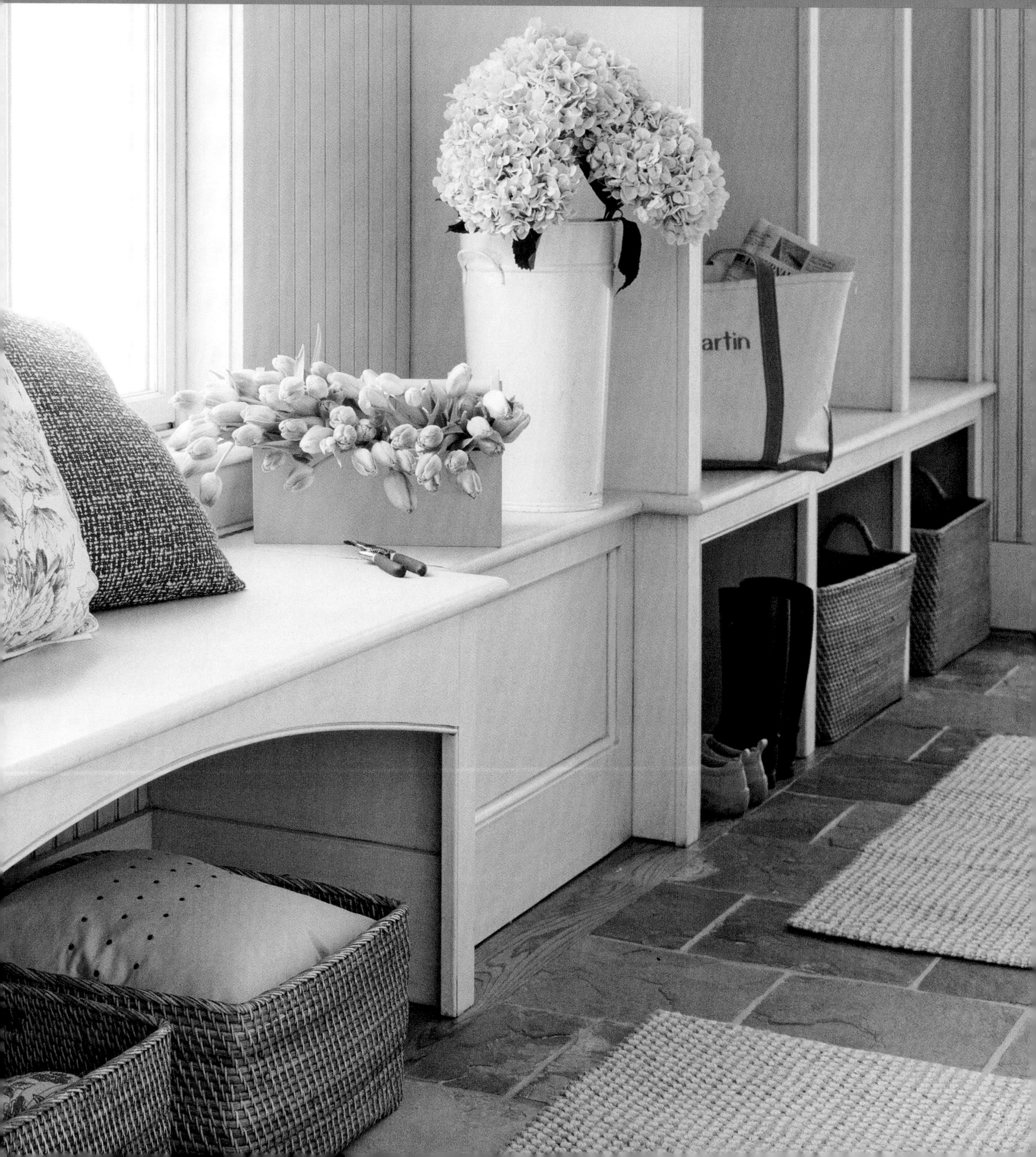

Tame the Routine

The secret to organizing mudrooms and entryways is to catch the clutter before it makes its way into the rest of the house. Think of the first thing each family member does when stepping inside the front door: Drops the keys, dumps the bags, and kicks off the shoes. Even in tight spaces, the right furniture and organizational tools can make it as easy to put these items away as it is to drop them on the floor.

Install a shelf equipped with a couple of baskets to catch keys and cell phones. Use a pretty jar to contain loose change. Install hooks to hang up coats and add a bench with cubbies for taking off and stashing shoes. In a few hours' time, you can transform a dumping ground into an organizational zone that welcomes family and guests alike.

This custom-built divider catches all the gear that comes through the front door and keeps the floor clear of clutter. Shelves and cubbies are sized to hold a week's worth of gear.

A narrow ready-made storage cabinet can fit in a tight space and organize everything from balls and backpacks to watering cans and clay pots.

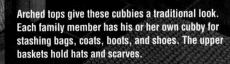

Arched tops give these cubbies a traditional look. Each family member has his or her own cubby for stashing bags, coats, boots, and shoes. The upper baskets hold hats and scarves.

Corral the Clutter

Eliminate the entryway and mudroom mayhem with these quick tips for organizing family supplies:

• Keep everyday items within easy reach—it makes coming and going a much quicker and easier process.

• If you opt for built-in storage, make sure the design you choose can keep up with your child's and family's needs.

• If your entry is short on space, place a bin for each child near the stairs or hallway that leads to the bedrooms.

• Install a chalkboard by the back door and write notes and reminders in a print large enough to draw attention.

• Put a basket on the kitchen desk to serve as a drop-off point for important school papers.

• Give everyone a hook at his or her height to make hanging up coats effortless. Install additional hooks for backpacks, sports bags, purses, and the dog's leash.

This drawer-filled cabinet doubles as a bench seat. The drawers feature nameplates so that family members can quickly stash what they need as they come and go throughout the day. Select furnishings like these that perform more than one duty.

This backdoor entrance connects to a hot tub and swimming pool. Cubbies above the bench provide storage for towels and other outdoor essentials.

The top of this window seat opens to provide storage for stadium blankets and other weekend gear. The window seat is located adjacent to the coat cubbies, opposite.

HOW TO MAKE A WOODEN-HANGER COATRACK

This backdoor entrance doubles as a pet center and provides storage for dog food, pet bowls, and other supplies. The tiled shower stall is great for cleaning muddy paws, boots, and shoes.

Put your wooden hangers to work in a new way: Use them to create a pretty and functional coatrack. Attach shortened hangers to a 1×4 as shown by screwing the hangers in place on the backside of the board.

Attach the coatrack to the wall by mounting heavy-duty picture hangers onto the back of the 1×4. Space the picture hangers so that you can attach the rack to wall studs.

Install a drain by the back door and let boots, umbrellas, swimsuits, and other wet items drip dry—no puddle cleanup required.

At this backdoor entrance, high and low storage enables kids and adults to help themselves to what they need. Put all of the available space to work.

Lined baskets tucked inside a closet keep this combination mudroom and laundry area neat. A stacked washer and dryer provides the space for the storage closet.

❧ Keep It Clean

Your laundry room may be a dedicated room or it may share space with a basement, mudroom, bathroom, or kitchen. Whatever the case make it a pleasant area to work by creating a specific place for stashing dirty clothes and hanging and folding clean ones. If you have the space, install a flat counter-height surface for sorting and folding laundry, then add a shelf above the counter for stashing supplies. If space is limited, you can fold clothes on top of the dryer. When installing shelves above the washer, be sure to allow enough space for opening and closing the machine's lid.

Baskets are ideal for eliminating piles on the floor—make sure they are open-weave to allow air to circulate. A wall-mounted drying rack that folds back into place is another practical addition. Leftover cabinets from a bath remodeling or a rolling caddy and some wire shelving can fill a need.

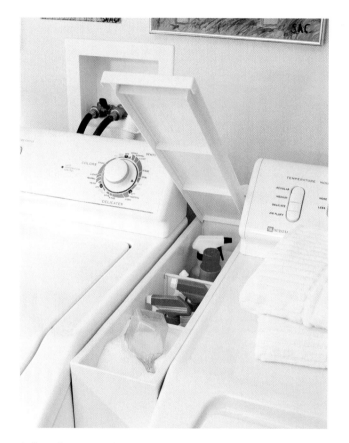

A sliver of space provides convenient storage. This storage caddy tucks between the washer and dryer.

Purchased from a home center, this freestanding cabinet holds a laundry basket for each family member.

Every Inch Counts

If your laundry area is limited to a small closet, use the open space above the washer and dryer to sort colors into canvas bags hung across a closet rod, as shown on page 47. Give the closet an extra design dash by painting the walls a favorite color.

If your washer and dryer are housed in a guest bath or the garage, consider hiding the machines behind bifold cabinetry doors. As a space-saving alternative, invest in a stackable washer and dryer and tuck them inside a ventilated closet. Use the extra floor space to create a storage closet complete with shelves and organizers.

Store supplies such as carpet cleaners and spot removers in plastic baskets or bins so you can easily transport them to the trouble spots. A chest of drawers is an excellent storage addition: Apply stenciled labels so everyone in the family knows what is stored inside.

CLUTTER BUSTERS

Piles of clothing, bottles of detergent, and laundry baskets can quickly take over a laundry area. To keep things in order, plan multiple types of storage. Here are a few essentials to keep in mind:

- **Find room for an ironing board.** Install a pull-down ironing board that's built into a cabinet or door. You can also find easy-to-install racks that hold the board at home centers and hardware stores.
- **Include shelves or cubbies.** Use open storage to keep detergents and fabric softeners within easy reach. Open space below a counter provides a spot to tuck laundry baskets and sorters out of the way.
- **Include space for clothes that need to air dry.** Install a closet rod above a utility sink or between wall-hung cabinets.

Glass cookie jars show off the colors and textures of spare sponges and laundry additives. Labeled drawers store spare linens.

This stylish room makes doing laundry a favorite chore. The large vessel sink is perfect for soaking hand washables.

A combination of open shelves and cabinets organize this laundry center. A sink and folding counter increase the efficiency of the room.

Mudroom and laundry areas are ideal for storing pet foods and feeding bowls. This pullout bin stores large bags of kibble.

Embroidered laundry sorters make functional and attractive use out of the space above the washer and dryer.

Built-in cabinets (some with etched glass doors) lend a designer element to this combination mudroom and laundry area.

 # Laundry Armoire

This classy laundry center is an ideal addition to an apartment or second home. Start with an unfinished wood cabinet (sold at unfinished furniture stores). Fill any dents or dings in the wood with wood filler and let dry. Sand the surfaces lightly and wipe with a tack rag. Then stain or prime and paint as desired. Because the cabinet is in a high-moisture environment, top the paint or stain with one or more coats of a clear sealer, such as polyurethane.

This cabinet's interior, opposite, is as attractive as its exterior. Pretty baskets, boxes, and jars keep detergent, bleach, fabric softener, and other mundane supplies within easy reach.

HOW TO CUSTOMIZE A LAUNDRY ARMOIRE

Turn an unfinished piece of furniture into an armoire that neatly stores everything you need for laundry day (except the washing machine).

1. Give the cabinet a one-of-a-kind look by color washing the door insets and crown molding a soft shade of blue or your favorite color.
2. Customize the interior with handy wire racks you can screw into the doors or place on an existing interior shelf. In either location the racks put spot removers and ironing supplies in plain view and within easy reach. Install a whiteboard for jotting down to-do lists.
3. Add a tote basket that allows you to take all the laundry supplies to the washing machine in one trip.
4. Repurpose ready-made organizers to store what you use most. In this armoire a former belt-and-tie organizer screws into the inside of the right door and holds fragrant sachets. A shower caddy attached to the opposite door holds soaps and fabric fresheners.
5. A cotton bag slung over the door is just the thing for holding clothespins neatly. The strap slips over your shoulder when it's time to haul the clothes basket outside to the line.
6. A spacious bottom section of the armoire—created by removing some shelves—is ideal for storing a folded drying rack and canvas hampers. When the ironing is done, hang the folded board on a hanger mounted on the armoire's exterior.

A pickled and color-washed finish combines with old-fashioned door pulls to make this cabinet the perfect addition to a classic cottage-style home.

HOW TO REMOVE STAINS

TUESDAY
wash whites

WEDNESDAY
ironing

SUNDAY
hand wash delicates

BLEACH

detergent

cedar balls   soap   fragrance

MORTON
Speediwash
MORTON INDUSTRIES · CHICAGO

COLORS   WHITES

This laundry armoire tucks into the corner of any room: a guest or master bedroom, bath, gathering area, or hallway.

Dining Areas

Dining spaces are the perfect place to connect with family and friends and enjoy the simple pleasures of food and conversation. Whether your dining place is a formal room or a casual locale off the kitchen, make the most of the area with storage solutions that enrich the look of the room.

Match Style and Storage

To determine the amount of storage you need, think about how you entertain and what would make mealtime more convenient. Perhaps a place to store china, flatware, glasses, linens, and serving pieces would be a benefit. Or maybe you would prefer a storage piece that also provides buffet service.

Once you know what you'd like to store in the room, survey your existing furniture. Do you have an antique armoire or contemporary chest that could provide extra storage and/or an extra serving surface? Adapt an existing cabinet to your needs by lining a drawer with fabric and adding dividers for silverware storage. Vertical dowels added to a cabinet interior make it easy to store and retrieve serving trays. Drawers equipped with dividers, as shown on page 55, organize plates, bowls, and serving pieces.

This antique cupboard look-alike is narrow enough to fit in the wall space behind French doors and extends the full length of the room.

Custom-built, this storage piece provided the opportunity for perfectly sized display space to accommodate an extensive collection of antique Dutch, French, and English transferware pieces.

Put Wasted Space to Work

If you will be purchasing or building new furnishings for the room, incorporate additional storage in underutilized areas. For instance you might use a storage cabinet as a table base or install drawers beneath a window. If you have the space, separate the dining area and kitchen with a half-wall containing a built-in sideboard, as shown on pages 50–51. A compact corner cupboard or simple open shelves create storage in a small space. A ready-made plate rack also works great in a dining room—you can store and display your favorite china in minutes.

As you plan, remember it's often more interesting to mix rather than match. In the dining area on pages 52–53, a custom-made painted cabinet fills a once empty wall with storage and looks extremely attractive next to a vintage wooden table and chairs.

A stylish wine rack serves as the base for a built-in table. This granite-topped rack is constructed from maple strips and complements the kitchen's cabinets.

Movable pegs organize plates and bowls in this built-in dining hutch.

A basic closet is transformed into a customized storage unit with the addition of shelves and drawers. This closet features shelves for storing plates, glasses, and serving pieces, and drawers for storing table linens and silverware.

MORE IDEAS FOR DINING ROOMS

Implement these tips in the dining room for storing dishes, glasses, and linens.

- In a deep drawer install evenly spaced wooden dowels parallel to the drawer front. Neatly fold and drape tablecloths and other linens over the dowels for minimal creasing.
- For long-term storage of heirloom dishes, cut cardboard rounds to suit the size of the plates. Layer one round between plates to prevent chipping.
- Install special racks on the bottoms of cabinet shelves to hold stemware upside down so dust stays out.

Flat pullout drawers keep a variety of linens wrinkle-free and organized. Sort your linens by function—napkins, runners, tablecloths, placemats—or color.

If you live in an apartment or simply want storage that's easy to relocate to another room, use a freestanding shelf unit that requires minimal floor space. The one above is easy to build and customize to any height or configuration.

Freestanding Shelves

The clean lines of this pipe-and-plywood shelving unit make it suitable for any style of dining room, and it fits neatly into a corner or against a wall. You can also construct a lower version to set beneath a window. The unit shown here has alternating open rectangles for glassware and other goods, and cubes with crisscross dividers for stowing wine. As an alternative install vertical dividers for plates or horizontal shelves within cubes for folded linens.

HOW TO BUILD FREESTANDING SHELVES

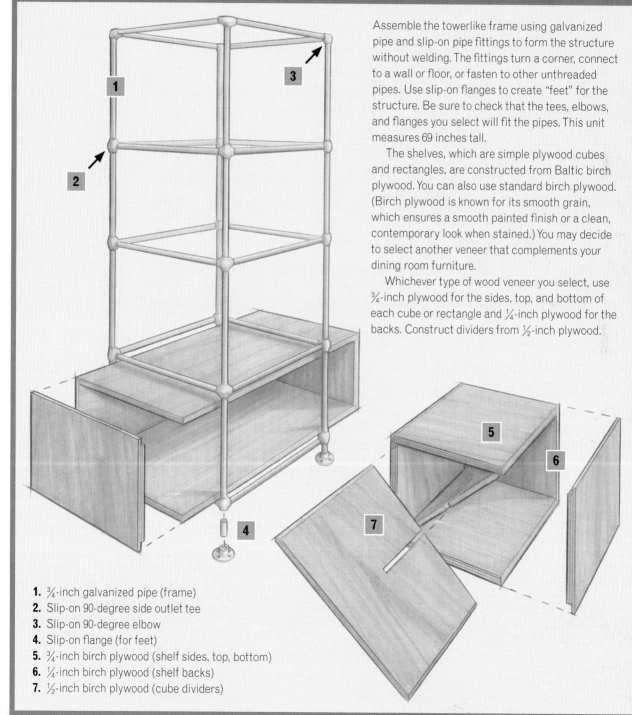

Assemble the towerlike frame using galvanized pipe and slip-on pipe fittings to form the structure without welding. The fittings turn a corner, connect to a wall or floor, or fasten to other unthreaded pipes. Use slip-on flanges to create "feet" for the structure. Be sure to check that the tees, elbows, and flanges you select will fit the pipes. This unit measures 69 inches tall.

The shelves, which are simple plywood cubes and rectangles, are constructed from Baltic birch plywood. You can also use standard birch plywood. (Birch plywood is known for its smooth grain, which ensures a smooth painted finish or a clean, contemporary look when stained.) You may decide to select another veneer that complements your dining room furniture.

Whichever type of wood veneer you select, use ¾-inch plywood for the sides, top, and bottom of each cube or rectangle and ¼-inch plywood for the backs. Construct dividers from ½-inch plywood.

1. ¾-inch galvanized pipe (frame)
2. Slip-on 90-degree side outlet tee
3. Slip-on 90-degree elbow
4. Slip-on flange (for feet)
5. ¾-inch birch plywood (shelf sides, top, bottom)
6. ¼-inch birch plywood (shelf backs)
7. ½-inch birch plywood (cube dividers)

4 Living, Family

By day the family room serves as a recreation hub for the kids. At night the same area becomes a media center and family gathering place. The living room provides a spot for entertaining family and friends or curling up with a good book. The goal in organizing these gathering spaces is to keep everything in a convenient place while maximizing the aesthetics of the room.

& Media Rooms

◾ Organized Living

If you are tired of the clutter on your coffee table or have trouble finding the remote on a regular basis, rethink the storage strategies you use in your gathering rooms. To up the organization level, find a logical place for everything, even for the items you use every day.

To keep books, magazines, remote controls, and other living room accessories from straying, group them in baskets, bowls, or holders specifically designed to organize these items.

Maximize storage capacity and minimize clutter with built-in cabinets designed to hold all of your media equipment and more. Choose furnishings that offer extra storage, such as side tables fitted with storage drawers, ottomans that open to hold blankets and pillows, and chests that hide toys and games.

To keep the room looking great every day, spend a couple minutes each evening putting things away.

The modern media equipment in this stylish living room disappears behind the closed doors of a custom armoire that was designed to look centuries old.

Floor-to-ceiling open shelves bring the fireplace wall to the forefront. Different-size cubicles ensure an organized, visually appealing display. Baskets keep clutter under wraps.

STYLE AND STORAGE

- **Measure the items you need to store.** Plan your tallest shelf to fit the largest item and space the other shelves to hold smaller accessories.
- **Increase your display space.** Layer art and collectibles in changeable, eye-pleasing ways.
- **Mix and match.** Sprinkle a few pretty accessories between matching storage boxes and baskets.
- **Repeat.** Items of the same size and color look less cluttered than a conglomeration of mismatched books and accessories.
- **Double up.** Choose accessories that offer more storage. Pieces of vintage luggage easily stack up to side-table height. Ceramic canisters look great and keep small items out of sight.

Storage solutions can be simple. Hang wooden cubes on the wall to organize books and CDs. A lamp entices readers to sit.

Sleek flat-front cabinets hide the TV and cable boxes. Open cubbies make it easy to select a DVD.

Media Room Magic

Storage for media can be sleek and beautiful or rustic and charming. Whatever style you choose, make sure it will hold the size and number of items you have—or plan to have soon. (TVs don't last forever, and it's likely the next one you bring home will be larger and thinner than the one you own now.) When designing a built-in media center, consider where and when sunlight enters, so you can avoid as much glare on your TV screen as possible. If you prefer to keep your equipment out of sight when not in use, choose armoire-style doors that pull out and tuck in on either side of the TV. That way the open doors won't block sight lines or walkways. Plan for cords, power outlets, and ventilation, ideally through the back of the unit, and make sure you can view the television screen from multiple spots in the room.

Drawers are handy for stashing DVDs, multiple remote controls, and games—both electronic and board-style.

This simple built-in unit fits below a window and closes when you want to hide the television.

Flat-front maple doors render a sleek look appropriate for a media center. Large pullout drawers combine with additional cabinets to keep electronic media and equipment out of sight.

ORGANIZE YOUR ELECTRONIC MEDIA

- Transfer tapes onto DVDs. You'll reduce the amount of storage you need and be able to donate your VCR to a favorite charity.
- Group CDs and DVDs by category and genre, or organize them alphabetically by title, and place them book-style on shelves so their titles are evident.
- When investing in DVD storage, think long-term. Look for ready-made units that offer flexible shelving that can grow and change along with your collections.

This wall-hugging storage unit wraps the corner of the room and makes use of every inch of available space. The storage shelves are meticulously spaced to hold each electronic component.

Literary Collections

The most enticing home libraries contain books that are artfully displayed and easy to reach. Books are aesthetically pleasing when mingled among photos and mementos. If space is at a premium, create visual interest by stacking some books horizontally instead of vertically to render room to perch an accessory or two. Fashion an air of organization by placing books of the same size together, generating a neater, more uniform appearance. If color coordination tops your list of priorities, consider wrapping the books in two or three shades of decorative waxed papers.

To streamline a mix of magazines and books, consider purchasing color-coordinated magazine holders to mingle amid the books.

Bookshelves surround French doors and put the architecture of the house to good use.

Combine ready-made shelves to organize an
entire library of books.

REDUCE THE PAPER PILES

- If you are receiving magazines you don't read,
  cancel the subscriptions. Instead of saving
  whole magazines, clip articles and recipes and
  tuck them into plastic sleeves stored in a binder.
- Keep only the catalogs you order from;
  toss old catalogs the day you receive the new
  copy in the mail.
- Group magazine holders together on the
  shelf, then allow some open space between the
  holders. The relief areas provide a resting place
  for the eye and a good place to display a few
  attractive accessories.

Shelves and fine cabinetry show off books and collectibles.
Lighting installed below each shelf produces a warm glow.

This innovative rack organizes newspapers and magazines and puts empty wall space to work.

HOW TO BUILD A MAGAZINE RACK

This mega-size rack—a maple frame fitted with ½-inch EMT thin-wall electrical conduit—provides a stylish way to organize magazines and newspapers. Lean the rack against the wall nearest to your favorite reading chair. If you have small children in your home, attach the top of the frame to the wall studs using a sturdy metal hook-and-eye fastener.

1. Frame. You can build any size, of course, but the rack shown is 70 inches high and 42 inches wide, built from 2×6 maple lumber. Have a hardwood retailer mill the maple down to 1½ inches thick and 5 inches wide, with edges and faces straight and parallel. Also have the shop cut the mitered ends for the rails and stiles. For help aligning the surfaces so they are flush, cut ½-inch deep slots as shown so you can glue splines into each corner.

2. Hanger tubes. Mark the hole locations for the hanger tubes. Designate the ends you want at the bottom, then measure from the inside of the miter and draw light pencil lines at the 15-, 29-, 43-, and 57-inch marks. Drill a hole at each mark, to a depth of about 1¾ inches. Use a hacksaw to cut the metal tubing into 35-inch lengths, then file the cut ends to remove any sharp edges.

3. Assembly. Working on top of a drop cloth, glue the entire assembly together, then put a pipe clamp across the top and bottom ends to pull the corners tight. Let the assembly set overnight, then finish the wood as desired—the unit shown has two coats of dark penetrating oil. Let the finish dry for at least 24 hours before hanging any magazines.

A small wooden ladder leaned against a wall organizes magazines and newspapers in a family room. Mirrored tiles next to the ladder are framed in wood stained to match the ladder. Mirrors make the small room appear more open and spacious, which reduces visual clutter.

Home Offices

A home office provides a place to pay the bills, surf the net, answer emails, work from home, and everything in between. Dedicating a specific place in your home—whether it's a room or a portion of one—to accomplish these tasks will help organize your busy life and reduce the piles of paper clutter that tend to gather on counters and tabletops throughout a home.

Divide and Conquer

If your current office has become a catchall for clutter, make the task of organizing it more manageable by dividing the space into manageable chunks. A good strategy is to organize your filing cabinet first, then file the papers that have gathered on the desktop. File only what you really need to keep—if you aren't sure, talk to an accountant. On average more than half of what Americans file is never looked at again. If you can access the necessary information by making a phone call or visiting a website, you may be able to shred the papers instead of filing them. Clear off open shelves next. Doing so provides instant gratification because you can see the progress you've made. Use paper organizers, baskets, and vertical files to easily access what you need while making the shelves appear less cluttered and more attractive.

White binders establish a uniform appearance on open shelves. A basket organizes smaller items, and a floral bouquet infuses color.

The stylish desk above is actually file cabinets covered with fabric panels and topped with glass.

The owner of this home office only has to climb the stairs to commute. Inexpensive open shelves organize notebooks and reference materials. A wing chair, purchased from a consignment shop and covered with silk remnants, provides comfort for guests.

Baskets organize the desktop. A table runner adds unexpected color and design dash.

Plan Ahead

Allow enough filing space for all of your paperwork and include enough spare storage to keep yourself organized for several months. Consider using rolling cabinets that you can move to another area, such as a nearby closet, when the files they contain are no longer active. To prevent paperwork pileups, spend a few minutes at the end of each workday tidying up the space.

Make paying bills a simpler task by keeping the bills, envelopes, and stamps within reach of where you write the checks and file the stubs. If your bank offers an online bill-paying service, consider signing up—it is quicker than filling out forms and mailing them.

Ambience is also important. You'll be more likely to use an office you find attractive and inviting. Furnish your office space with a desk that is large enough for all your activities and arrange the surrounding storage so that what you use every day is within arm's reach. Paint the walls your favorite color and use attractive knickknacks and photographs to decorate.

PAPER CONTROL

Don't let mail and bills pile up. Take a few minutes each day to toss out the junk, shred sensitive items, and open the bills. Create a folder or dedicate a mail slot for the bills and review them weekly.

Don't print out every file and email. Instead take advantage of computer storage by establishing a regular electronic backup system.

A fabric-covered bulletin board is a pretty place for posting cards, flyers, phone numbers, and memorabilia.

Covering a basic office chair with a botanical print fabric softens its look and makes the perfect complement to the fabric-draped desk.

Dedicate Space

If space is limited in your home, think creatively. As shown on pages 70–71, a dining area can double as an office with the installation of open shelves and storage drawers along the walls. A small closet can be converted into a home office with the addition of a desk, wall-mounted shelves, and a door-mounted storage caddy.

To make a small space look organized, choose pastel colors for each of its components—light colors reflect light and create an illusion of spaciousness. Choose storage organizers that match. A row of four identical baskets, for example, looks less cluttered than a trio of different size and shaped ones.

A closet is just the right size for a small home office. At the end of the day all the papers, equipment, and clutter recede behind closed doors.

Set up a command center in a corner of your kitchen. Position the desk outside of the main traffic area and ideally below a window for visual inspiration. For a cohesive look, fashion the desktop from kitchen countertop material and the drawers from cabinets that match those in the kitchen. Recess shelves into an adjacent wall.

DRAWER ORGANIZATION

To streamline your desk drawers, empty and refill the drawers one at a time and organize the contents by category (such as client projects or insurance papers). Use the most accessible drawer (typically the top center one) to organize office supplies such as paper clips, sticky notes, scissors, rubber bands, a letter opener, and a few pens and pencils.

Open shelves and a wall-mounted computer desk transform a corner of the family room into a home office and a place for the kids to do homework.

❧ Turn Vertical Space into Storage

A bulletin board is a great spacesaver and allows you to display important information without cluttering your desktop. You can post daily reminders, receipts, and to-do lists where they are easy to see. Size your bulletin board to hold the items you would like to display. In the office opposite, sheets of corkboard have been mounted onto the wall, covered with fabric, and crisscrossed with ribbons for an attractive organizer that runs from floor to ceiling. Meld storage and display by showing off family photos between business-oriented items.

You can also put the other vertical surfaces in your home to work. Sides of cabinets, armoires, desks, and the tops of hutches can be fitted with hooks, brackets, wire baskets, and other organizers designed to hang on the wall.

HOW TO BUILD A FABRIC WALL BULLETIN BOARD

1. Corkboard. Purchase enough corkboard (available at home centers) to create the bulletin board you desire. If you want to cover an entire wall, as shown, start at the top corner of one of your office walls and nail sheets of corkboard in rows to cover the entire wall, trimming the last rows to fit.

2. Fabric and ribbons. Cut fabric to fit the length and width of the wall. If necessary sew strips of fabric together to achieve the width you need; hem edges. Starting in the same corner you started with the corkboard, staple the fabric onto the wall in 2-foot intervals. Cover the staples with crisscrossed ribbons held in place with tacks, as shown.

Option: For a puffier, softer appearance, add a thin layer of cotton batting between the cork and the fabric.

Turn the sides of your desk and other cabinets into storage magnets. Hang metal strips on the sides and use magnetic clips to keep keys and bags handy.

Other wall-mount organizers and accessories include in/out baskets, mail sorters, and calendars.

6 Master Bedrooms,

It's important that a master bedroom be a restful retreat. Too much clutter and untidiness, and you'll dwell on all the work to be done instead of the relaxing you should be doing. Use these solutions to ensure that your bedroom and related storage areas are calm and composed, so you can be too.

Dressing Areas & Closets

Suite Storage Sensation

Take stock of all the belongings you want to reside in your master bedroom. Books, a television, a DVD player, DVDs, a stereo, and CDs are the most-listed items that people want stored in their den of personal renewal. The challenge is keeping all these things accessible without overwhelming the room. Designating wall space for floor-to-ceiling storage and display is one way to gain organizational opportunities without sacrificing style. Plan for a combination of open shelves for books and treasures and closed cabinets for concealing media gear or other items that you want out of sight.

If your master bedroom has a fireplace, allocate the flanking wall space for shelves or, better still, tall cabinets with doors to hide the television, stereo, and related gear. Select doors that complement other woodwork in the room and that open and slide back into the cabinet to fully reveal the television screen. (Refer to the manuals that come with your television, stereo, and DVD player to ensure that the cabinet cavity provides an adequate ventilation area around the equipment.)

Media equipment is only one set of measurements you should know. Be sure to measure bulky belongings (coffee-table books, pottery, and artwork, for example) and plan storage that offers an adequate depth and height to accommodate these things.

Tall doors on each side of this master bedroom fireplace have the visual effect of a handsome paneled wall. Closed storage removes any sign of clutter and appoints the fireplace as the focal point.

The doors open and slide back inside the cabinet to reveal a combination of drawers, open shelves, and another cabinet. The built-in storage provides ample space for media equipment as well as for CDs and DVDs.

CONQUER BEDROOM CLUTTER

- **Help with hobbies.** If you find yourself knitting or pursuing other hobbies from bed, group the related paraphernalia in a basket that stashes under the bed.
- **Organize the nightstand.** If you must keep pills, tissues, or a glass on the nightstand, group them all in a decorative tray. Containers instantly lend the surface an air of neatness.
- **Free up floor space.** Mount a nightstand on the wall (see page 97 for instructions), or integrate it into your headboard (see pages 80–81 for one sleek example).
- **Add a bench.** At the end of the bed, add a trunk or storage bench as an extra location for storing blankets, pillows, and books.

Open shelves in a sunny corner forge the quintessential reading spot that's invitingly furnished with a chaise. The built-in beneath the window volunteers a cabinet with a display ledge on top.

A storage wall divides this spacious walk-in master closet. On the end of the wall, a large mirror abuts a cushioned bench (with baskets below), making the closet as much about dressing as it is about storing clothes. Reflected in the mirror a cabinet with slanted open shelving keeps shoes in order and easy to see.

Dream Closet Closeups

Time is usually at a premium when you're getting ready for work or an event. No one wants to spend precious minutes digging through a disastrous closet to find the clothing and accessories needed for an outfit. It takes only a few days of planning and sorting through your things to come up with an ideal master closet design. The reward will be a gorgeous, well-organized storage space and a more relaxed morning routine.

First measure the length and height of the closet walls and take the dimensions to a specialty closet store. These retail outlets are often willing to provide free closet diagrams and help you select the components to achieve the plan. Inform the consultant of special storage needs, such as large collections of handbags or footwear.

You can also visit online closet component stores. (Some Internet search terms include "closets," "closet designs," or "closet planning.") Many online sites offer free closet planning. Typically you click on your closet type (reach-in, walk-in rectangle or square, or odd-shaped walk-in) and input the dimensions of each wall. A customized closet design appears on-screen featuring a collection of storage components that you order through the site.

While you're waiting for your new closet pieces to arrive, sort clothing and accessories. Put items you haven't worn in a year in an "out" pile. Toss anything that's stained or in poor condition and donate the rest to charity.

As you store items in the new closet, organize them by type, color, and season. Stow out-of-season clothing up high (keep a step stool in your closet) and put the pieces you wear frequently at easy-to-reach heights.

An abundance of drawers accommodates everything from socks to sweaters. Open cubbies above the drawers offer quick access and an instant inventory of folded tops. Closed cabinets at the top of the walls house out-of-season items. Dual rods double the usable hanging space within the adjacent alcove.

Dream Closet Closeups

If your master bedroom lacks a spacious walk-in closet that you can outfit as an organizational dream, consider your options. This combination dressing room/ master bedroom closet was made possible thanks to an extra bedroom adjacent to the master bedroom and across from the master bath. The generous amount of floor space allowed for an island, a handy component for laying out clothing and packing for trips. All of the storage elements in this room are custom-fit to meet the homeowners' needs and painted white for a light and airy feel.

An uninterrupted wall and center island make this master closet—once an unused bedroom— ideal for dressing. The combination of drawers, cubbies, and hanging rods offers an abundance of storage options.

Larger niches are good for welcoming, colorful decor, such as this pot of flowers. Shoes and handbags fill smaller cubbies.

No need to purchase clear plastic shoeboxes when you use this labeling trick. Take a photo of the footwear you plan to store and attach the print to the end of the box. You'll always know which pair is where, plus the boxes stack and store easily on a shelf.

Wrinkled clothes can put a hitch in your morning routine. Smooth your schedule with an ironing board in the dressing room. This one pulls out from the end of the island, which also features drawer storage.

❧ A Clean Solution

It's not how much space you have available in the bedroom, it's how you put it into play. If you have an average-size master bedroom but crave a large collection of clothing and clean-lined design, a storage wall could offer the ideal solution.

The master suite below packs abundant storage and style into a modest space. By slightly moving the bedroom door, the designer was able to create an entire wall of storage. In keeping with the homeowners' love of simplicity and an uncluttered environment, the wall is an uninterrupted facade of flush maple doors, drawers, and filler panels with nearly invisible hardware. With doors closed it offers the warmth of simple wood panels.

Inside, an organizational dream of shelves in a variety of heights stands ready. The assorted storage components are custom-sized to accommodate clothing, accessories, and an entertainment system.

For visual continuity one cabinet door works as an entrance to a spacious walk-in closet, the result of merging two smaller closets. Complementary maple cabinetry continues into an adjoining dressing room that furthers the uncluttered style.

Opening the door panels and drawers along the wall reveals an abundance of storage as well as a home for the television. The door on the right opens to a walk-in closet.

The space this tall cabinet occupies was originally the bathroom entry. Relocating the door freed up the opening for more built-in storage.

When closed the continuous light maple panels lend a warm, spacious feel to the room.

The master bedroom's headboard matches the closet doors. A low chest of drawers furthers the maple theme and provides storage for magazines, books, and bedtime necessities.

The dressing room cabinet is truly multipurpose. Upper shelves store linens and towels. The middle door flips down to reveal a desk niche that includes a fax machine. The bottom drawer is a laundry bin.

Simple Solutions

Part of the fun of organizing and customizing your master bedroom closet is finding specialty storage features that meet your needs spot-on. Stroll the storage aisles at the home center, investigate the goods at a specialty closet retailer, or cruise online closet stores, and you'll discover an almost endless array of clever containers, organizers, and ideas. The gallery of savvy storage solutions below puts to work some available options.

This "shoe mobile" holds clear shoeboxes, so shoe options remain in view. To make one, purchase a plastic, two-shelf storage cube. Equip a laminate board base with casters and mount the cube to the board. Place pairs of shoes inside each shoebox and stack the boxes.

Ties can become a tangle unless you provide a spot to keep them in view and organized. In the stackable wooden drawer divider *above*, each cubby provides enough space for two neatly rolled ties. Another option is the floor-based cabinet *below*, which opens to reveal a pair of neckwear-wielding rods that swing out for easy access.

Storing business suit pieces in one location eases the morning routine. In this closet several rods multiply hanging space and keep coats and shirts above eye level, pants below, and full-length items to the side.

Socks stay put when the drawer is divided into neat sections just right for one pair. This plastic grid adjusts to fit various drawer sizes. Other options include spring-loaded metal dividers or interlocking boxes.

When your closet includes a flat surface for folding clothes, you're more likely to keep shirts and sweaters neatly stacked.

Incorporate a foolproof storage method such as cubbies and tap into an almost automatically well-kept shoe collection. Ready tomorrow's outfit on an extension valet, i.e., a handy pullout hanging rod.

A deep pullout bin makes a great built-in hamper. Use one to keep your dirty clothes off the floor and out of sight.

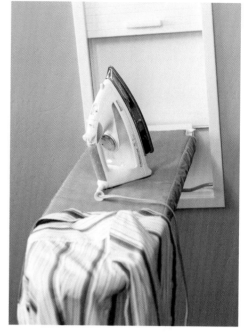

Wherever there's clothing there's bound to be wrinkles. This ironing board folds away in a wall unit until you need it.

Fill a closet from front to back by eliminating the need for pulls or knobs on the built-in drawer fronts. These sleek drawers feature cutout handholds instead of hardware. To re-create this unit, have a cabinetmaker install drawer glides in a stock cabinet and make drawers as deep as possible to fit behind the door.

Long scarves are a fabulous fashion accessory but a challenge to store. This pullout solves the dilemma: Wooden dowels mounted in a drawer keep a colorful collection of scarves arranged in tidy rows.

Window of Opportunity

Old houses are long on character and notoriously short on closet space. Whether or not you live in an old house, your bedroom could likely benefit from additional closets. One way to gain closet space in an existing bedroom is to bump into an adjoining room or borrow a few square feet from a wide hallway. Consider, too, the area that surrounds a bedroom window. Wall space above, below, and to the sides of the window all have the potential to be valuable storage. This bedroom window features a storage bench below, an open shelf above, and tall flanking closets, thus providing cozy seating and ample storage in one attractive unit. Now the once-wasted wall is an ultrafunctional focal point.

A window seat such as this one contributes several practical bonuses: The closets and storage bench keep the space clutter free while the cushioned top makes the room seem even more cozy and comfortable. The bench is also a handy spot to put on shoes.

HOW TO BUILD WINDOW SEAT STORAGE

The window seat and built-in storage ensemble is large in scale, but it involves simple construction techniques that most novice woodworkers can manage.

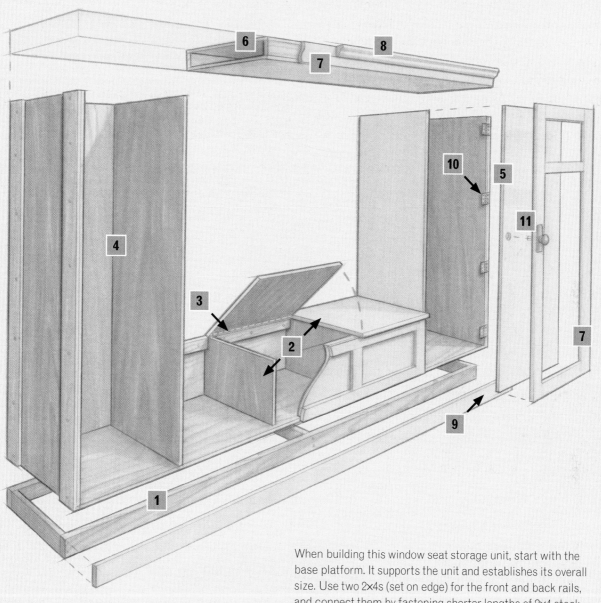

1. 2x4 base
2. ¾-inch plywood panels (bench sides and top)
3. Piano hinge for bench tops
4. ½-inch plywood (closet sides and backs)
5. ¾-inch plywood (closet doors)
6. 1x4s (frame for boxed soffit shelf)
7. Iron-on veneer tape
8. Decorative molding
9. ½-inch trim (recessed panel effects and fascia for boxed soffit)
10. No-mortise hinges for doors
11. Door knobs

When building this window seat storage unit, start with the base platform. It supports the unit and establishes its overall size. Use two 2x4s (set on edge) for the front and back rails, and connect them by fastening shorter lengths of 2x4 stock at the ends and center. The base should be about 2 inches shallower than the 16–18 inches of depth for the bench and cabinet assemblies; the length can vary according to the window size and your needs (keeping it under 8 feet will allow you to cut the base panel from a single length of plywood). Shim as necessary to level the base platform. Secure the cabinet backs to the wall, making sure the cabinets don't twist as the screws are tightened. Join lids (tops) to the bench using piano hinges. Also use iron-on veneer tape to dress up the edges of the door panels. Use glue and 4d finishing nails to fasten ½-inch-thick trim to the doors and to the bench front. Apply decorative molding to the soffit frame. Finish the unit with paint or stain and let dry, then attach hinges and knobs.

❀ Bedroom Bonuses

Those in need of new full-size closets must think big. One option is to replace a wall between the bedroom and bath with a pair of closets that serves as attractive privacy dividers. This design centers the entry to the bath for attractive symmetry and a clear delineation between his and her closets. The units below were custom-built using plywood and beautiful wood veneers for a contemporary look. A pair of bedside tables was built to match.

The lower portion of each closet features a bank of drawers and reserves plenty of room for hanging clothes above. Drywalling the walls between closet dividers establishes a short hallway that leads into the bathroom.

HOW TO BUILD A NIGHTSTAND

This compact design provides support for a bedside lamp and other items, plus a drawer for discreet storage. The version shown here features an exterior of wood veneer and high-pressure laminate applied to a wood substrate.

If you want to include the lamp cord grommets, remove the drawer and drill a 1⁹⁄₁₆-inch hole near the back edge of the top panel. Drill a corresponding hole through the bottom panel (working from below) to route the electrical cord, then fit the grommet into the hole in the top panel. Route the lamp cord through the holes, then replace the drawer.

1. ¾-inch birch plywood
2. ¾-inch birch veneer tape
3. 1×3 poplar
4. 10-inch full-extension drawer slides
5. Lamp cord grommet

A sleek, rectangular nightstand is suspended from the wall on each side of the bed and offers a nearly invisible drawer for storage. The floating design allows a look at the floor below and thereby remains visually open.

Bathrooms

The best baths make the beginning and end of each day as stress free as possible. Up your bath's efficiency level with one-step storage that can save you precious moments each morning and night. Increase the room's storage capacity by making the space you have work harder and by finding additional space that you can quickly put to work.

The Ultimate Storage Bath

If you are building or remodeling a bath, carefully plan the storage to meet the needs of each family member who will use the room. A husband and wife might connect the bath to his-and-hers closets so they can enter the bath in pajamas and exit dressed and ready for the day. Take advantage of empty walls by installing built-in cabinets or open shelves. Equip the vanity base with pullout drawers that enable you to see and reach everything—even items in the very back.

Consider placing the toilet and shower in a separate closet so that one individual can privately use those components while another washes at the vanity. Plan enough storage for towels, shower soaps, and toiletries. Save steps by installing a clothes chute that connects to a lower-level laundry, or better yet, move the laundry area to a room next to the bath.

Three tilt-out bins tuck into the tub's deck and make great laundry or towel bins. For extra luxury, bath towels hang on a heated rack.

The shower's glass enclosure is a good choice for a small bath; it keeps the space visually open. A built-in ledge and shampoo niche keep supplies nearby.

Window seats, vanity benches, and tub surrounds are ideal areas in which to infuse drawers and bins. Here tilt-out bins keep fresh towels under wrap and close at hand.

The vanity's flared drawers render added floor space in this small bath without giving up much storage capacity. Long, narrow cabinets below each sink offer a place to stash cleaning supplies.

Narrow cabinets turn the wall space between vanity mirrors into efficient storage. The center doors above the countertop open to reveal sidelights that are ideal for applying makeup and shaving.

BOOST YOUR STORAGE CAPACITY

If you've employed every storage strategy possible and still find that your bath territory is too tight, scout out adjacent areas:

- Use the hall closet nearest the bathroom to store spare towels and supplies. Up the closet's storage capacity and neatness quotient with vertical dividers and storage cubbies.
- If possible steal a few feet of space from an adjacent bedroom, hallway, or closet. If you're lucky you may simply be able to add a door inside the bath that connects to an existing closet.
- If you can't spare any of the adjacent space, consider adding on. A 2-foot-wide bumpout along one wall provided enough area for the built-in shown on page 104.

Better Built-Ins

Increase the storage capacity of the vanity by choosing kitchen cabinets instead of bath cabinets for the vanity base. Vanity cabinets typically measure 32 inches high by 18 to 21 inches deep. Base cabinets designed for kitchen use feature a 36-inch counter height that most people find comfortable to use in the bath. The cabinets are also 36 inches deep, which nearly doubles the typical bath vanity. Utilize your bath's vertical space by running the built-ins from the floor to the ceiling. If you are more apt to put something away when you can see where it goes, consider glass doors and open shelves. If you prefer clean lines and a sleek appearance, hide your things behind solid doors.

Instead of closing in the bath pantry, open it up. Here a combination of glass shelves and roomy drawers service a room that's as pretty as it is practical.

This distinctive vanity stores everything in the open for quick retrieval.

Frosted glass doors pair with colorful cubbies to store towels, soaps, washcloths, and even a few spare pillows.

A bench furnishes a place to land while you pull on socks and shoes. It also doubles as storage when it contains a flip-down door or pullout drawers.

Open shelves become a colorful display when filled with rolled towels in complementary colors.

TOWEL STORAGE

A stack of fluffy towels makes guests and family members feel welcome. Roll and stack them vertically inside a deep, round basket or stack them on top of the tub deck. For a pampering touch, replace a basic metal towel rack with an electric towel warmer—just be sure you have a place where you can plug it in.

This built-in hutch comes with extra counterspace and a nook for stashing hand towels.

You Can Take It With You

Take a furniture approach to your bathroom's storage needs by using freestanding pieces you can buy or build. The storage is ideal for rental homes because you can take the pieces with you when you move.

For reasons of flexibility choose ready-made pieces with movable shelves you can arrange to fit your personal gear. Maximize the interior storage capacity by installing pullout bins below each shelf. Meld style with organization by using painted wicker baskets adorned with fabric liners to hold less attractive fare, such as hair ties and styling brushes. Display stacked towels in complementary colors and relegate the faded ones to the garage. Show off soaps and bath salts in pretty clear containers.

A metal shelving unit becomes an attractive and commodious storage piece with the addition of matching baskets and canisters. Coat hooks put open wall space to work.

This vintage steel hospital cabinet *above* tucks between two trough-style sinks and provides storage for a variety of necessities.

The small glass-front cabinet (*top right*) is the kind of piece you can find at a furniture store. It fits against any open wall and organizes everything from toilet paper and cotton balls to spare towels.

Taking the doors off of a stand-alone storage cabinet (*right*) makes it easy to find what you need. The interior blue ups the appeal. Glass jars, wire racks, and baskets ensure order.

Slide-out wire bins (*below*), available at storage stores and home centers, organize small items, such as washcloths and tea towels.

 # Linen Closet

Remove items that you use only once or twice a year, such as spare blankets and old sheets, and store them in a less convenient spot, such as in a box under the bed or inside a spare bedroom closet. Then put the space you dedicated to those items to better use. Boost the capacity of your linen closet by putting all the wasted space to work. Use baskets to organize small items, and install half shelves, which make it easier to reach specific items without having to sort through tall stacks. Use vertical dividers to compartmentalize the space and consider installing pullout shelves in closets that are extra deep.

For a more organized appearance, group like items together and use smaller baskets to divide the drawer space.

HOW TO CUSTOMIZE A LINEN CLOSET

Start with a new freestanding cabinet or adapt these ideas to a hall closet. Whichever you choose, follow three easy steps.

1. Divide the shelves with wooden corbels, sometimes called brackets. Position the corbels to support stacks of folded towels and linens. Apply wood glue between the back of the corbel and the cabinet wall. Use screws to secure the lower side of the shelves to the corbels.

2. Label the shelf edges to designate which size sheets or towels go where. To make the shelf edges more attractive, hot-glue ribbons onto them. These letters, commonly used on mailboxes, were purchased from a home center and attached on top of the edge ribbon with hot glue.

3. Install basket-style drawers on runners so that the baskets easily slide in and out. Depending on the size of the cabinet, you may need to install a vertical dividing board to support the runner near the center of the shelf. Use screws to secure the board to the bottom of the cabinet and the top of the board.

Simple brackets secured to the shelf help hold linens in neat stacks. Metal-letter labels on shelf edges designate what goes where.

In just a few hours' time you can equip an existing cabinet or hall closet to store bath linens and toiletries.

❀ Recessed Wall Cabinet

If your bath has empty wall space, it has room enough for a tall, narrow cabinet that slides in between the studs. Also consider an easier, though less attractive, fix: open shelves between the studs.

Before cutting into the drywall, review your home plan to check for the placement of plumbing lines and electrical wiring. This cabinet is made from cherry wood to match the other cabinets in the bath, but you can use any quality hardwood. Customize the shelf sizes to meet your individual needs.

Aluminum rails hold rolled towels in place. Half shelves organize small toiletries.

Recessed into the stud wall, this narrow cherry cabinet takes up only a few inches of floor space.

HOW TO BUILD A RECESSED CABINET

If you have basic carpentry skills, you can make this cabinet in a weekend's time.

1. Side panel
2. Fixed shelf
3. Stud cheek
4. Stud cap
5. Back panel
6. Side filler
7. Top filler
8. Frame stile
9. Frame rail
10. Half ledge
11. Adjustable shelf
12. Rod blocks
13. Door stile
14. Door rail
15. Door panel

Before building the cabinet, cut away the wallboard or plaster opening to locate and measure the exposed studs and the distances between them. The inside contours at the center of this cabinet are designed to fit into a conventional stud-frame wall, with 2×4 studs spaced at 16 inches on center. You'll need to modify the cabinet design if your walls are built to different measurements.

Cut the cabinet parts using the illustration as your guide. To assemble the column for the center stud, glue and nail the stud cheek and the stud cap together, with ends flush as shown.

Purchase semicustom cabinet doors in the size you need or make them as illustrated. Follow the hinge manufacturer's instructions for drilling holes on the inside of the door frames but before installing the hinges, test-fit the doors and if necessary trim the edges slightly to provide clearance gaps for opening and closing.

Apply stain and finish, allowing drying time between coats. To install the cabinet, insert it into the wall cavity until the back edges butt up against the wallboard. Attach the cabinet by screwing several drywall screws into the studs through the side panels. Make sure the cabinet remains square and flat so it fits properly. Next install the cross rods and rod support blocks. Recruit a helper to hold the doors in place while you fasten the hinges to the frame stiles. Adjust the fit once all doors are installed, then drill holes for the knobs and install.

8 Kids' Spaces and

Shoes, clothes, toys, books, **CD**s, school materials, and games are the kind of belongings that contribute to messy kids' rooms. You can thwart the problem by putting the following smart storage solutions into practice. While you're at it, transform your extra bedrooms into storage havens that also comfortably accommodate overnight guests.

Guest Rooms

✿ Personalized Storage

You've heard the old adage time and again, but that doesn't make it any less true: Children need a place for everything in order to learn to keep everything in its place. Consider the gear you find strewn about your kids' rooms most often, and you have a starting place for selecting the personal storage needed to corral all their things.

Your primary goal, of course, is to get it off the floor and hopefully in an organized manner. One common thread among kids is that they like to see their belongings. For that reason a big, solid toy box is often an unsuccessful storage strategy because items are out of sight and jumbled together. Instead try several clear plastic bins so your child can sort and see what's inside.

Another fun option is to hang a 12-pocket over-the-door clear vinyl shoe organizer. Your child can use the slots for small toys, art supplies—or even shoes! If the storage containers you choose are opaque, label the contents so children who read know what goes where. For younger kids put a picture of what's inside on the outside of the box. Better still, provide open shelves for a few favorite toys and games so these remain in full view but off the floor.

ADAPTABLE CABINET

An armoire is a freestanding piece you can use to store and display your child's things. Hot-glue painted corkboard to the interior sides and back of one door to devise a

Built-in drawers hold larger items and are labeled accordingly. If your child doesn't read, use decoupage glue to adhere a photo clipped from a magazine.

Translucent bins on pullout platforms allow children to get a good look before grabbing. Plan carefully before buying bins: Inventory belongings, then purchase those that fit what your child needs to store.

quick-change gallery for graded papers, friends' photos, or artwork. Coat the inside panels of the other door with chalkboard paint. If the inside of the cabinet you purchase is flat, simply cover the borders with painter's tape before painting. Encourage craft activities by providing easy-to-reach roller paper: Install eye hooks beneath the top shelf; hold paper on a dowel cut about 4 inches longer than the roll.

Use plastic containers to hold school supplies and chalk, and include a clear bin for additional supplies and belongings. Reserve the top shelf for games, books, and toys used less often and make the bottom bins home to daily favorites.

HOW TO CUSTOMIZE A CABINET

Paint an unfinished computer cabinet white and add colorful containers that you can change as your child grows (or whenever you're ready to redecorate). Equip the inside with:

1. A desktop for homework and art projects
2. Labeled drawers for toys and supplies
3. A bar for holding a roll of craft paper
4. An open shelf for games and toys
5. Painted corkboard surfaces for displaying artwork
6. Chalkboard surfaces for drawing and writing
7. A horizontal slot for storing poster boards and papers
8. Cube storage for holding bins and divided containers

Tied shades brighten a wall of three cube storage and display towers. When lowered they conceal belongings.

Clutter Control for Play Spaces

Readily accessible open shelves encourage kids to keep clutter under control in a playroom. Clean-lined cube-style shelves especially lend themselves to quick cleanups. Provide enough cubes so that every toy, game, and book has a spot off the floor. Add bins that fit on the shelves (or beneath seating areas) for sorting and holding smaller belongings, such as interlocking blocks, dollhouse furniture, and action figures. Label one or more cubes for each child, so everyone who uses the room has personal storage space. Have them store favorite items on lower shelves and things they play with less often on upper shelves. Establish an evening routine that involves siblings in a playroom pickup time. Done daily, an average-size playroom can be brought to order in about 5 minutes.

DECLUTTER WITH CUBES

Build as many cubes as you need and stack several in symmetrical towers, experiment with stair-stepped or other creative configurations, or simply line a row of cubes along a wall.

Birch plywood is a good option for building these cubes because it offers subtle graining that ensures a clean look for a stained finish or a smooth painted surface. One 4×8-foot plywood sheet should provide enough material for seven 1-foot-square boxes.

When determining the cube size you wish to build, measure the thickness of the plywood you purchased. (Plywood thicknesses can vary.) Then factor in the thickness as you determine the lengths of the sides, top, and bottom.

Assemble the cubes using wood glue and 4d finishing nails. Fill the exposed edges with wood putty and paint to finish, or finish exposed edges with wood veneer tape.

HOW TO BUILD STORAGE CUBES

Simple painted or stained wood boxes, or cubes, are attractive and easy to make. This trio of cubes are constructed from ¾-inch birch plywood.

Bins—painted metal, such as the ones under the bed, or plastic—work well on shelves or slipped beneath a seating bench or crafts table for "hidden" storage.

Busy Minds and Hands

Dedicating a space to homework and handiwork, such as crafts and other artistic pursuits, keeps the kitchen table clear of clutter. In fact, a space such as this can work hard for every member of the family, not just the children.

Figure out how much work surface you'll need for comfort. For example, if your child uses large poster board for paintings, you'll need a large work surface. You'll also need enough desktop to accommodate multiple children doing homework.

Keep in mind that plenty of shelves, drawers, good lighting, and comfortable seating are all important design decisions.

Containers that slide into precise position make sorting and finding supplies a snap, while shallow drawers are the perfect spot to store large tablets of paper.

Use space below work surfaces for positioning additional storage cabinets. Keep belongings down low for smaller children. Open shelves can hold books and games.

A built-in cabinet such as this one holds multiple storage bins. If space is too tight, outfit a closet or purchase a rolling cabinet with drawers.

Clear plastic containers let you see what's inside. Long, shallow drawers are ideal for storing large papers or poster board.

Guest Rooms Plus

Unless you have lots of extra space in your house, you'll probably want your guest room to serve dual purposes. Of course you'll want to ensure that overnight visitors are comfortable by including storage they can use during their visit. But you can also equip closets and the bedroom space for your own organizational needs.

Provide a nightstand for each side of the bed. Keep in mind that it may hold an alarm clock, a telephone, eyeglasses, a lamp, reading material, and perhaps a beverage and medications. Select a stand or low cabinet that suits the height of the mattress and that offers shelves, drawers, and/or cabinet storage.

Plan underbed storage for this room as well. Use low containers or drawers on rollers that will fit beneath the mattress to hold seasonal items and other lesser-used belongings. Another option is a vacuum-seal storage system that pulls the air out of large plastic storage bags and flattens bulky items such as pillows, comforters, and sweaters. These bags make it easier to store items beneath the bed and help you get more out of the capacity of your closet.

For visitors staying more than a few nights, include a chest of drawers; reserve one or two drawers for guests and use the remainder for storing linens and other goods.

Closets need hanging space and extra hangers for your guests' clothing as well as for your out-of-season clothes. Closet shelves outfitted with some baskets accommodate other household storage requirements.

A BETTER GUEST CLOSET

Use these five elements to make your reach-in guest closet an organizational bonus for your household.

1. A vertical storage tower takes advantage of closet space from top to bottom. A unit with one or more drawers is even more useful.

2. Closet bars—high and low—provide hanging space on each side of the storage tower. Allocate one side for guests and the other for your out-of-season clothing.

3. Baskets fit on shelves for keeping smaller items tidy.

4. An undercabinet fluorescent light eliminates shadows that conceal what you're searching for.

5. Cedar boards line the closet and emit a natural scent that repels insects. Kits containing enough planks for 15 square feet are available at home centers.

The days of a single closet rod with a shelf above are gone. Today even guest closets work much harder with the addition of well-chosen components that make better use of the space.

For a clean, uncluttered appearance, this built-in headboard extends beyond the sides of the mattress to offer handy bedside shelves.

Shelves and Sleepovers

The addition of built-in bookshelves may be all it takes to convert an extra bedroom into a combination library (or office space) and guest room.

Open shelves are ideal for books, framed photos, and treasures. If your budget allows, have the built-ins constructed with base cabinets for concealed storage that complements the room's woodwork. Use these cabinets to hold such items as photo albums or archive boxes and binders containing household records.

When storing books, provide enough shelf space so the volumes have plenty of room. You should be able to grasp the book by the spine, not the loop at the top, so you won't damage the binding.

Vertical wall space makes a guest bedroom/library possible. Floor-to-ceiling built-in shelves display a book collection in an attractive manner. Twin beds mounted on casters abut the shelving units and easily wheel away from the wall when needed.

BOOKSHELF BASICS

- Build a low corner bookcase with smoothed edges for safe and accessible storage. Measure what you plan to store before you design and install shelves.
- Plan for adjustable sizes rather than standard symmetrical arrangements. (Measure some bigger, oversize books to ensure that the shelves are of adequate size.)
- Consider weight loads. Architects often specify ¾-inch-thick birch plywood for bookshelves; spans should be no more than 36 inches between supports. If you use ½-inch plywood, reinforce it with supports every 24 inches.

A table between beds features beautiful storage boxes that suit a guest bedroom environment and are ideal for holding writing materials and other small items.

Traditional moldings make built-in shelves as beautiful as they are useful. Install crown molding at the top of freestanding shelf units to join separate pieces and fashion a built-in look.

9 Special Spaces

Once you have organized all the other rooms in your home, focus your attention on the secondary spaces—the messy garage and underused area below the stairs. Turn the page for terrific ways to make these small spots ultraefficient and organized. You'll also find ideas for establishing dedicated activity zones. Think crafts or sewing station, gardening center, and a beverage zone.

Organize the Garage

If your car has been ousted from the garage, it's time to clear the clutter and bring it back in. Start by figuring out what needs to be organized and what needs to go. Group items by activities: sports, lawn care, auto maintenance, home repair, gardening, and so on. Measure the length and width of the garage and your car(s) to determine how much space you can spare and still get the vehicle in the garage. Then purchase or build enough storage cabinets, shelves, hooks, and racks to organize the items by category, so that only large machinery and bulky items take up space on the floor. The storage units need not be expensive or complicated—a piece of particleboard, slightly bowed and attached to cornering walls with a 1×4 and screws, for example, serves as a great ball or toy bin.

If space is limited consider building a backyard shed for additional items—or build an addition with a second overhead door onto the back of the garage and keep the mower and other heavy-duty lawn care items in the new room.

Wall-mounted ribbed panels install in minutes and are designed to hold a variety of organizers including hooks, tool holders, and wire baskets.

This wall storage arrangement organizes tools and provides a handy workbench. Locks on cabinets keep chemicals out of the wrong hands.

RESTORE ORDER

Bring order back into your garage by following these simple steps.

1. Pick a sunny day to pull everything out of the garage.
2. Sort the collection into piles that correspond to your activity zones: gardening, sports, and so on.
3. Group smaller items in stackable plastic containers or tubs and label the holders and the shelves where you plan to stack them.
4. Get bikes and golf clubs off the floor with hooks and stash garden and lawn tools on racks designed to to organize these items.
5. Lock up any dangerous chemicals or supplies, such as paint and pesticides, in a heavy-duty cabinet.
6. Except for lawn mowers and other heavy equipment, vow to keep the floors clear of clutter.

These hooks attach to grooves on wall panels—no holes required—making it easy to rearrange items.

Pullout wire baskets enable you to easily reach items stored in deep bins. Hang cabinets a little higher on the wall to make room for a rolling cooler.

❀ In Plain Sight

Hooks and holders mounted on pegboard or slatwall panels are good, simple solutions to store tools in a garage. They get things off the ground, plus you can easily see what you need. The pegboard can be installed above a workbench or base cabinets, or below wall-mounted shelves and cabinets. The slatwall panel in the garage, opposite, is installed above a utility sink. If the ceiling in your garage is generous, consider building a sturdy loft above the overhead door. Then use this out-of-the-way space for stashing seasonal items. To make cleaning the garage an easier task any time of year, hang a paper-towel holder and organize cleaning supplies inside a nearby wall-hung wire basket.

This storage armoire holds everything needed for boating or a day at the shore. Organizing by activity makes it easier to quickly gather what you need and return items when you're done.

Step Up the Storage

If you have reworked your bedroom closets and reorganized your cabinets and you're still in need of storage space, take a walk through your home and brainstorm how you can make the space you have work harder.

Give your coat closets a makeover: Install storage shelves—or half shelves—above the hanging rods. Hang a shelf a foot off the floor to double your shoe storage.

If you have pictures hanging on the wall that you are not particularly fond of, replace them with open shelves, a plate rack, or a pair of wall cabinets. Have you tapped into the space underneath and beside the staircase? If possible

tear out a section of the drywall and replace it with recessed open shelves, or line one wall of the finished stairwell with storage cubbies to show off your family pictures, cherished collectibles, or a prized book collection.

The key to organizing a home is to make every space work harder—and to dedicate a few minutes of every day to put things back in their proper place.

Bookshelves along one side of the stairwell step up your staircase's storage potential. Placing the planks at every other step prepares the shelves for even the tallest of books.

Open shelves below the staircase showcase family photos. These stairs lead to a loft above a child's room—the loft keeps the toys off the floor of the main bedroom.

Just for You

If you have a beloved hobby, consider making a small portion of an underutilized room, such as a guest bedroom or formal dining room, into a hobby center. The wrapping station, opposite, lines a basement wall. It would work equally well in a mudroom, home office, or walk-in pantry.

Customized armoires also make excellent hobby centers. Open the armoire when you're ready to work and close it before guests arrive. For ideas on customizing a garden armoire, see pages 136–137. For ways to transform an armoire into a beverage center, see pages 138–139. If you don't spend enough time crafting to turn a piece of furniture into a hobby case, organize your gear in plastic totes you can easily transport from room to room. Store the tubs on shelves or at the back of an infrequently used closet. If you like to craft in the family room, consider organizing the necessary supplies inside pretty matching baskets you can display on shelves.

A vintage desk becomes a sewing center when equipped with fabric, thread, and needles. A closet dowel rod becomes attractive wall storage when cut to size and attached with corbels. Clear plastic storage jars hang on ribbons threaded through a pair of holes drilled into the lids.

This craft center handles everything from wrapping presents to mending clothing. Wall-mounted holders for ribbons and paper store the materials crease free.

Garden Storage

This armoire, below and opposite, looks beautiful inside a screen porch, a mudroom, or even in a corner of a kitchen, bath, or laundry area. Start with an unfinished wood cabinet and fill any dents or dings in the wood with wood filler and let dry. Sand all the surfaces lightly and wipe with a tack rag. Paint or stain the piece to complement the decor of the room.

If you'll use the cabinet in a high-moisture environment, top the paint or stain with one or more coats of polyurethane or your favorite clear sealer.

With a few simple changes, this ready-made armoire became a storage dream for any flower or vegetable gardener.

HOW TO CUSTOMIZE A GARDEN ARMOIRE

Choose an armoire large enough to hold all the items you want to keep on hand for gardening in the space allotted.

1. The top shelf holds garden-variety terra-cotta pots that have been painted. Secure a paper-towel holder under the shelf for quick cleanup.

2. Pegboard (from a home center) is an ideal backdrop for tool storage. Loop-style hooks keep trowels and garden claws in place.

3. Cut a canvas shoe organizer in two and use half to organize plant markers, gloves, and other essentials. Add ties to the other half to create an apron; it can travel from armoire to garden around your waist.

4. A galvanized metal shelf is both sturdy and durable enough for potting. You can order sheet metal cut to size from a home center.

5. Storage drawers hold everything from gardening books and magazines to knee pads and hats. Remove one drawer and use baskets to store bulbs and seeds.

A trio of metal bins hold soil and fertilizer.

A metal shelf is perfect for potting. A new pegboard backing organizes tools.

NEW YORK COCKTAIL

- juice of 1½ lime or ½ lemon
- 1 lump sugar
- 2 dashes grenadine
- A twist of orange peel
- 1½ ounces whiskey

The armoire looks as attractive open as it does closed.

Dedicated Beverage Center

You can find an armoire like this one at most furniture stores. This finished piece, originally part of a bedroom set, was designed to hold a television and other media equipment. If you prefer to finish the armoire yourself, shop at local stores or Internet websites that specialize in unfinished furniture.

HOW TO CREATE A DEDICATED BEVERAGE CENTER

1. Many armoires sold as media centers include a high shelf for a DVD player or cable box. Repurpose this space for the storage of tumblers. Suspend martini glasses and other stemware from a slotted rack screwed into the bottom of the high shelf. Ready-made slotted racks are available at home centers.

2. A ready-made storage shelf attached to the back of the armoire holds towels and displays drink garnishes.

3. Attached to one door, hooks and wire shelves organize drink-mixing tools. A large wire shelf attached to the back of the cabinet holds bottles and an ice bucket. Chalkboard paint converts the other door into a menu or recipe center.

4. A pullout shelf provides a place for mixing your favorite concoctions.

5. Remove the armoire's bottom doors and install a ready-made wine rack or create crisscross dividers from veneered plywood as shown on page 57. To the right of the wine rack, pullout shelves present recipe books and serving bowls.

Originally designed as a television armoire, this furniture-store find was repurposed into a decked-out beverage storage unit.

A wooden rack attached below an existing cubby provides the means for storing stemmed glasses.

 # Resources

At a Glance
800/365-9327
www.ataglance.com
Planning products, calendars

Bed, Bath & Beyond
800/462-3966
www.bedbathandbeyond.com
Storage and home organization products (Product line varies)

Bodum
800/232-6386
www.bodum.com
Kitchen storage products

Broadway Panhandler
866/266-5927
www.broadwaypanhandler.com
Knife storage

California Closets
888/336-9709
www.calclosets.com
Custom home storage systems

Casabella
800/841-4140
www.casabella.com
Storage and home organization products

CD Storehouse
800/829-4203
CD storage products

The Container Store
888/266-8246
www.thecontainerstore.com
Storage and organization products

Crate & Barrel
800/967-6696
www.crateandbarrel.com
Storage and home organization products

Exposures
800/222-4947
www.exposuresonline.com
Photo display and storage products

Filofax
877/234-2426
www.filofax.com
Calendars, daily planners, and binders

Frontgate
888/263-9850
www.frontgate.com
Storage and home organization products

Garnet Hill
800/870-3513
www.garnethill.com
Home storage products

Gempler's
800/382-8473
www.gemplers.com
Tool storage solutions

Gracious Home
800/338-7809
www.gracioushome.com
Storage and home organization products

Hammacher Schlemmer
800/321-1484
www.hammacher.com
Home organization products

The Home Depot
800/553-3199
www.homedepot.com
Home organization and improvement products

IKEA
In the United States: 800/434-4532;
in Canada: 888/932-4532
www.ikea.com
Storage solutions and furniture

The Ink Pad
212/463-9876
www.theinkpadnyc.com
Personalized ink stamps

Itoya of America
800/628-4811
www.itoya.com
Home office organization products

Kitchen Accessories Unlimited
800/667-8721
www.kitchensource.com
Designer kitchen accessories and storage solutions

Levenger
800/667-8034
www.levenger.com
Reading and home office accessories

Light Impressions
800/828-6216
www.lightimpressionsdirect.com
Archival products

Lillian Vernon
800/901-9402
www.lillianvernon.com
Storage and home organization products

Museum of Useful Things
800/515-2707
www.themut.com
Home organization products

OfficeMax
800/283-7674
www.officemax.com
Home office organization and storage products

ORG
800/562-4257
www.homeorg.com
Home organization solutions

Organize.com
800/600-9817
www.organize.com
Organization products for home and office

Poliform
888/765-4367
www.poliformusa.com
Home storage products

Pomegranate
800/227-1428
www.pomegranate.com
Calendars

Pottery Barn
888/779-5176
www.potterybarn.com
Storage and home organization products

Racor
800/783-7725
www.racorinc.com
Garage storage solutions

Restoration Hardware
800/762-1005
www.restorationhardware.com
Home organization products

Rubbermaid
888/895-2110
www.rubbermaid.com
Storage and home organization products

Stacks & Stacks
800/761-5222
www.stacksandstacks.com
Home, office, and garden products

Staples
800/378-2753
www.staples.com
Home office organization products

Talas
212/219-0770
www.talasonline.com
Archival storage

Target Stores
800/591-3869
www.target.com
Storage and home organization products

Tupperware
800/366-3800
www.tupperware.com
Kitchen storage products

Ultimate Home Storage
800/397-7566
www.ultimatechristmas.com
Archival and holiday ornament storage

Umbra
800/387-5122
www.umbra.com
Storage and home organization products

Walmart
800/925-6278
www.walmart.com
Storage and home organization products

Williams-Sonoma
877/812-6235
www.williamssonoma.com
Storage and home organization products

Z Gallerie
800/358-8288
www.Zgallerie.com
Storage and home organization products

❦ Index

Welcome Home

STANLEY COMPLETE
Built-Ins,
Shelves & Bookcases

- STEP-BY-STEP INSTRUCTIONS
- CUSTOMIZING TIPS AND IDEAS
- PROJECTS FOR EVERY HOME

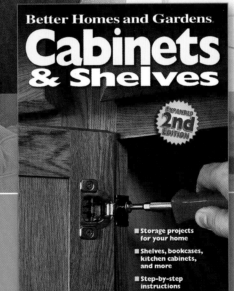

Better Homes and Gardens
Cabinets
& Shelves

EXPANDED 2nd EDITION

- Storage projects for your home
- Shelves, bookcases, kitchen cabinets, and more
- Step-by-step instructions

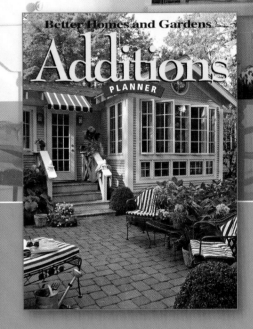

Better Homes and Gardens
Additions
PLANNER

Looking for **expert advice**, **inspiration**, **ideas** and **How-Tos** for **adding storage** and **organizing** your home?

Look for these and other Wiley titles wherever home improvement books are sold